Women, Nurturing Outlook and Ecology: Theory and Practice

Edited by Dr. Sangeeta Sharma

WOMEN, NURTURING OUTLOOK AND ECOLOGY: THEORY AND PRACTICE

Edited by

Dr. Sangeeta Sharma

Setu Publications
* Pittsburgh, PA (USA) *

We would be pleased to receive email correspondence regarding this publication or related topics at setuedit@gmail.com.

ISBN-13 (paperback): 978-1-947403-10-9
Printed and bound in the United States of America.
Distributed to the book trade worldwide by Setu Publications, Pittsburgh (USA)

Setu Literary Publications, Pittsburgh, USA

WOMEN, NURTURING OUTLOOK AND ECOLOGY: THEORY AND PRACTICE

Edited by

Dr. Sangeeta Sharma

DEDICATION

Dedicated to my Dad, Shri Jugesh Chandra Sharma, for being the constant inspiration and motivator!

Acknowledgement

While reading and teaching Eco-feminism to under-graduate learners, I thought it should not be the end. With the fast deteriorating ecological balance and newer environmental issues surfacing each day, it was imperative to do more than mere teaching to yield the desired results -- to involve more people in a project that encourages expression, a dialogue, discourse and re-examination of different texts from the perspective that has come to engage the entire world-community.

First of all I would like to thank the managing editor and publisher of Setu bilingual journal, Anurag Sharma and Setu Publication House for his encouragement and support towards this literary-critical project.

I appreciate Dr. Jaydeep Sarangi for writing the preface. Let me acknowledge all my contributing friends: Dr. Rajshree Trivedi; Dr. Lakshmi Muthukumar; Dr. S. Sridevi; Dr. Shweta Tiwari; Dr. Ancy Eapon; Dr.Debarati Das; Dr. G.D.Ingle; Dr. B.V. Saraswathy; Dr. Nisha Nambiar; Dr. Shweta Salian, Dr. Dipika Kolambe and my sister-friend Roula Pollard who has written especially for this -- a memoir and poems.

The names of the deserving student-contributors also need mention: Tanmay Bhamre and Jahnvi Jadhav for their full-length papers; Ruchi Yadav for her graphics and Rashika Shaikh for her poetic compositions.

I thank Srishti, my daughter, who lovingly helped me in formatting and Toronto-based son, Sparsh, for his keen editorial insights.

I hope this slim volume acts as an academic resource to the budding scholars, researchers and critics in their academic pursuits and opens up new vistas of knowledge.

Happy Reading!

WOMEN, NURTURING OUTLOOK AND ECOLOGY: THEORY AND PRACTICE

Table of Contents

Preface

Packed with diverse range of essays by renowned scholars and writers from different parts of the globe, edited by a veteran academician, poet and critic Sangeeta Sharma, the present anthology reflects a genuine sense of self-critical logic and commitments while remaining universal in voice. The reader will hope to think on the truth, engaging it honestly and through enticing subjects. The spectrum of the book is wide and varied. Some essays are finely crafted moments of scholarship and research, and take us towards that compelling intersection of the commitments and honesty. A memoir, poetry section and graphic designs add fresh interest to the book.

Light within is our soul's weather. It grows intangibly, without our notice. Light is the ultimate we look for. It is the power within, a design of hardcore cultural fabrics. Entries in this anthology are record of deep-seated questioning minds carrying reverberations within. The essays in the volume cover a large cross section of concerns—society, politics, gender, culture, ecology, etc. In the age of climate emergency, the book works towards the goal of science as to provide a theory of nature, where man has not yet attained a truth broad enough to comprehend all of nature's forms and phenomena. When a man gazes at the stars, he becomes aware of his own separateness from the material world. The stars were made to allow him to perceive the "perpetual presence of the sublime." Our delight in the landscape, which is made up of many unique forms, provides an example of integrated vision.

The history of life on earth has been a history of interaction between living things and their surroundings. The poet, painter, sculptor, musician, and architect are all inspired by natural beauty and offer a unified vision in their work. Art thus represents nature as distilled by man. Unlike the uses of nature described in "Commodity," the role of nature in satisfying man's desire for beauty is an end in itself. Beauty, like truth and goodness, is an expression of God. Man enters in the kingdom of his own dominion over nature with wonder. We recall Emerson who discusses the poetical approach to nature.

Eco-critical and feminist discourses have strongly engaged for the case that women are closer to nature and this fact has been woven into the tapestry of art and writing. This book is a much-needed study and is an important addition to critical work in the area. Each page of the book is armed with love, fortitude and hope.

We hear gentle clicks.

Jaydeep Sarangi

Widely acclaimed bilingual poet-academic and translator anchored in Kolkata

Professor of English and Principal, New Alipore College, Kolkata.

15th March 2020, South Kolkata

Introduction

For more than two decades now, Eco-Criticism as a distinct domain has come to contribute new insights and awareness into the complex relationship between the earth, climate and humankind. Eco-critical writing and activism, of late, have come to dominate the collective consciousness and have triggered global conversations with great urgency.

The teen-sensation Greta Thunberg has put some honest and bold questions to the top political leadership of the world and has gained international recognition for promoting the view that humanity is facing an existential crisis arising from climate change. This collection of research articles and creative pieces continues the tradition of exploring this broad theme and global concerns.

The anthology is a right mix of theory, literary criticism and creativity. These contributors have raised some vital questions. Women play a major role in the ecology and the environment of a given area. Their nurturing capabilities are unique, and they have shown the world a way out through activism and conservation efforts. The Chipko movement was a grand success and similar movements have been witnessed across the world.

Right from time immemorial man has been changing the face of Nature and not always has he done it to the ultimate advantage of the earth or himself. Man has, in fact, destroyed more than necessary.

In his struggle to live and extract the most out of earth, man has destroyed many species of wildlife and also the forests. The process of excessive consumption of natural resources that started with industrialization has resulted in the depletion of these resources and greenhouse effect. The recent bushfires, hurricanes, drought and excessive rains testify to the present and clear danger of extreme climate change. We should wake up to the fact that if there is no earth there will be no life at all.

In the present anthology, senior academics and scholars have made an attempt towards re-reading of literary texts with an eco-feminist and eco-critical point of view and have found affinity between environment and literature.

Dr. Ancy Eapen's research throws light on the contribution of women towards conservation of ecology and biodiversity. It gives insight into the close interaction of women with nature that has been prevalent from olden times and which has remained unacknowledged, and sometimes ignored by patriarchy.

Dr. B. V. Saraswathy in her paper: Reading Arab Women's Literature through Intersectionality aims to analyse the intersectionality of religion, societal traditions and patriarchy in the novel *Celestial Bodies.*

Dr. Debarati Das analyses the writings of Temsula Ao and Easterine Iralu of the northeastern region. Temsula Ao through her poems shows the necessity to safeguard and nurture Mother Nature for our posterity.

Dr. Dipika V. Kolambe analyses the realistic contemporary features of native Nepal which influence and circumscribe the human life and its activities as portrayed in the second novel of Manjushree Thapa, *The Tutor of History* (2001).

Dr. (Smt.) G.D. Ingle, through her paper entitled: Ecological Concerns and Novelistic Art of Virginia Woolf's *The Voyage Out*, testifies Woolf's ecological concerns. She exemplifies how Woolf accords superior status to nature, portrays it as independent of human beings, humanizes Nature and demands that she be treated with respect.

Dr. Lakshami Muthukumar attempts to present eco-fiction as a genre that offers great potential for amateur writers of fiction.

Dr. Nisha Nambiar examines Kaveri Nambisan's novel *The Scent of Pepper* from a eco-critical point- of-view whereas Shweta Salian attempts to look at some of the female characters in Carter's fiction, *The Passion of New Eve*, to understand the manner in which she deconstructs established identities.

Dr. Rajshree Trivedi applies the principles of eco-psychology, a branch of psychology, to the reading of Mahasweta Devi's short stories anthologized in *Bitter Soil*.

Dr. Shweta Tiwari reconfigures ecofeminism by studying women characters in Anita Desai's *Fire on the Mountain*. Her paper seeks to foreground theoretical loopholes in ecofeminism and that the relationship between women and nature is not absolute but ambivalent.

Dr. S. Sridevi in her paper titled: Contemporary Women Nurturing Family in Urban Dwelling, Yoshimoto analyses the novella *Kitchen* as a metaphysical journey into sustenance and energy creation.

Roula Pollard, the eminent poet and environmental activist, also embellish this series. Overall, these are some of the enduring concerns and visions articulated by these scholars.

A lot has to be done in this expanding field.

In order to motivate and encourage budding poets and critics, debut research papers of the two young researchers, Tanmay S. Bhamre and Janhavi Jadhav, poems of Rashika Shaikh and graphics of Ruchi Yadav, all students of English literature have been anthologized in the present venture.

– *Sangeeta Sharma*

Editor, Mumbai (India)

Environment, Women and Political Ecology

- Dr Ancy Eapen

Bio: **Dr. Ancy Eapen**, department of English –PG, JGI, Palace Road, Bangalore; has thirty years of teaching experience in literature, specialized in Ethnic Literature; interested in Environment, Gender, and Culture studies, as well as child welfare.

Abstract:

The view of biodiversity produced by dominant institutions such as the World Bank, World Conservation Union, World Resources Institute and World Wildlife Fund, and supported by G-7 countries is based on a particular representation of the "threats to biodiversity" which emphasize loss of habitats, species introduction in alien habitats, and fragmentation due to habitat reduction. It fails to address the underlying causes, rather, it offers a set of prescriptions for the conservation and sustainable use of resources at the international, national and local levels; it suggests appropriate mechanisms for biodiversity management, including scientific research in methods of conservation. It also suggests economic use of biodiversity resources, chiefly through intellectual property rights. This dominant discourse is being actively promoted from a variety of sites and through manifold academic, institutional, managerial, and political practices.

The discourse of biodiversity as resource management is linked to three discourses: conservation science, sustainable development, and benefits sharing, either through intellectual property rights or through other mechanisms. Although there is great variation in the positions taken by national governments in the Third World, it can be said that there is a Third World national perspective that, without questioning the global-centric discourse, seeks to negotiate the terms of biodiversity treaties and strategies. This article looks into the strategy adopted by the Third World countries in acknowledging the logic of diversity as a holistic ecology and a more enlightened science than the bio-imperialism of global-centric perspective that advocates the logic of uniformity. The proposal for bio-democracy that ensues is articulated around a series of requirements that include: local control of natural resources, suspension of mega development projects and of subsidies to diversity-destroying- activities, support for practices based on the logic of diversity; redefinition of productivity and efficiency to reflect this logic; and recognition of the cultural basis of biological diversity. The research throws light on the contribution of women in ecological and biodiversity conservation. It gives insight to the close interaction of women with nature that has been prevalent from olden times and which remained unacknowledged, sometimes ignored by patriarchy.

Keywords: biodiversity, politics of ecology, women and environment.

Introduction

India has one of the highest rates of economic and population growth of all the developing countries. At the same time, it is also a country rich in biodiversity and culture. Consequently, it is difficult and yet imperative, to negotiate the delicate balance between development and nature conservation. Unfortunately, the focus of policy makers is veering more towards the country's economic development than to conservation of biodiversity. The idea of biodiversity first emerged in the 1990s with a master narrative of a biological crisis, which was launched at the global level in the 1992 Rio Summit. This narrative gave rise to constructions of particular discourses that hinged on the simple paradigm of threats and possible solutions. The aim was primarily to create a stable network for the movement of objects, resources, knowledge and materials. Within a few years, an entire network was established that amounted to what Brush (1998) called a tremendous "invasion into the public domain." However, the biodiversity network has not resulted in a hegemonic construction as it has been happening in other instances of techno-science. Alternative discourses produced by subaltern actors have emerged in the ecological debates and this has thrown up some interesting insights regarding deep ecology and the politics operating in this domain. Natural habitats, species conservation, as well as areas of tribal settlement should be preserved for the natural and ecological well- being of a country where natural resources, biodiversity and indigenous tribes still exist.

The history of life on earth has been a history of interaction between living things and their surroundings: human beings, flora and fauna have been molded by the environment. However, since the advance of science and technology from the nineteenth century, one species, the human being has acquired significant power to control and manipulate the natural environment for selfish interests. In the past quarter century this power has increased to a disturbing magnitude. The most alarming of all man's assaults upon the environment is the contamination of air, earth, rivers and sea with lethal and poisonous materials. In 2009, the United Nations General Assembly proclaimed 22 April as International Mother Earth's Day. The Member States acknowledged that the Earth and its ecosystems are [our] common home and expressed their conviction that it is necessary to promote harmony with nature in order to achieve a just balance among the economic, social, and environmental needs of present and future generation. In the same year the UN General Assembly adopted its first resolution on Harmony with Nature. Since then the UN Harmony with Nature report comes out every year, as a summary of the steps taken to achieve the objectives of the resolution. On 23 April 2018, the General Assembly in its eighth interactive dialogue discussed "Earth jurisprudence [1] in the implementation of sustainable production and consumptive patterns in harmony with nature." The U.N. secretary general's report on Harmony with Nature issued in conjunction with the conference, elaborates on the importance of reconnecting with nature as human beings are an inseparable part of nature and destruction upon nature will bring destruction upon human beings themselves.

Separatism is at the root of disharmony with nature and violence against nature and people. As the prominent South African environmentalist Cormac Cullinan points out, apartheid means separateness and humanity has been practicing eco-apartheid since a long time. The war against the Earth began with this idea of separateness.

Robert Boyle, a famous seventeenth century chemist and evangelist of New England wanted to rid the native indigenous people of their ideas about nature. He considered their perception of nature an impediment to the growth of humans over the 'inferior' creatures of God. This death-of-nature idea allows a war to be unleashed against the Earth, for the Earth is merely dead matter; there nothing is being killed. Its contemporary seeds were sown when the living Earth was transformed into dead matter to facilitate the industrial revolution. Monocultures replaced diversity. "Raw materials" and "dead matter" replaced a vibrant Earth. Terra Nullius (the empty land, ready for occupation regardless of the presence of Indigenous peoples) replaced Terra Madre (Mother Earth).This philosophy goes back to Francis Bacon, called the father of modern science, who said that science and the inventions that result would have the power to conquer and subdue Nature and shake her to her foundations.

In the 2018 UN General Assembly conference on Harmony with Nature, the Permanent Representative of India highlighted that understanding the interconnectedness of the Earth's systems had been present among early communities and indigenous groups all over the world. There were local practices to ensure the protection of the environment. However, a scientific outlook and the rapid technological advance had introduced an exploitative attitude of humans towards the environment. In order to restore the ecosystem, legal rights had to be conferred on natural entities.

Philosopher and historian Carolyn Merchant points out that the shift of perspective: from nature as a living, nurturing mother, to inert, dead matter to be manipulated, was well suited to the activities that would lead to capitalism.

Today, at a time of multiple crises intensified by globalization, we need to move away from the paradigm of nature as dead matter and move to a deep-ecology paradigm, and for this the best teacher is nature herself. The Earth University teaches Earth Democracy, which is the freedom for all species to evolve within the web of life, and the freedom and responsibility of humans, as members of the

Earth family, to recognize, protect, and respect the rights of other species. Earth Democracy is a shift from anthropocentrism to ecocentrism. And since we all depend on the Earth, Earth Democracy translates into human rights: to food and water, to freedom from hunger and thirst. The Earth University is inspired by Rabindranath Tagore, India's national poet and a Nobel Prize laureate. Tagore had started a learning center at Shantiniketan, in West Bengal, India, as a forest school, both to take inspiration from nature and to create an Indian cultural renaissance. The school became a university in 1921, growing into one of India's most famous centers of learning. In his essay "Tapovan" (Forest of Purity), Tagore wrote that the Indian civilization had become distinctive in locating its source of regeneration, material and intellectual, in the forest, and not in the city. Tagore believed that India's best ideas have come when mankind was in communion with trees and rivers and lakes, away from the crowds; the peace of the forest helped the intellectual evolution of man and shaped the culture of Indian society.

It is this unity in diversity which is the basis of both ecological sustainability and democracy. Diversity without unity becomes the source of conflict and contest. Unity without diversity becomes the ground for external control. This is true of both nature and culture. The forest is a unity in its diversity, and we are united with nature through our relationship with the forest. The forest teaches us union and compassion. It also teaches us satiety: as a principle of equity, how to enjoy the gifts of nature without exploitation and accumulation. No species in a forest appropriates the share of another species. Every species sustains itself in cooperation with others. The conflict between greed and compassion, conquest and cooperation, violence and harmony that Tagore wrote about continues today. And it is the forest that can show us the way beyond this conflict. The current scientific approach to biodiversity is focused less on theorizing and more on assessing the significance of biodiversity loss to ecosystem functioning.

Anthropologists, geographers, and political ecologists are demonstrating with increasing eloquence that many rural communities in the Third World "construct" nature in strikingly different ways than what is seen in the more modern and western societies. Ethnographic studies unveil a coherent set of practices of thinking about, relating to, and using the biological, and these local models do not follow the nature-society dichotomy. Unlike, modern constructions, with their strict separation between biophysical, human, and supernatural worlds, local models in many non-western contexts are often predicated on links of continuity between the three spheres and embedded in social relations that cannot be reduced to modern, capitalist forms. Recent anthropological approaches treat local knowledge as a "practical, situated activity, constituted by a past, but changing, history of practices" (Hobert 1993:17).This means that knowledge works through a body of practices than by relying on a system of shared context-free knowledge. This practice –oriented view of local knowledge has its origins in the theoretical positions taken by Heidegger, Bourdieu, and Giddens. For Ingold (1995, 1996) our knowledge of the world can be described as a process of acquiring skills from the practical engagement with the environment. All these trends signal a broader framework to which discussions of biodiversity conservation and related issues can be referred. This task is yet to be done in many countries across the globe, including India.

The biodiversity discourse has opened up a network which systematically organizes the production of epistemology and types of power, linking one to the other through concrete strategies and programs. There are international institutions, botanical gardens, universities and research institutes in first and third worlds, pharmaceutical companies and the great variety of experts located in each of these sites. Sometimes the 'truths' arrived at from any one site is resisted by social movements that become themselves the sites of important counter discourses.

Biodiversity has always existed as a natural process. But threats to biodiversity arise when the rate of extinction exceeds the rate of speciation. The losses in biodiversity is primarily caused by human interactions with the natural resources. In the early phase of civilization, humans remained a part of the ecosystem; but recently, humans have become a factor of the ecosystem and consequently started reshaping the biodiversity in such a way as to make it primarily a human sourced phenomenon. A brief look at some of the ways in which biodiversity has been appropriated by humanity would throw light on the magnitude and gravity of the problem.

Threats to biodiversity

These are the primary ways biodiversity is under threat:

1. **Habitat conversion/ fragmentation/ degradation**:

   Homogenization of certain species composition lead to a decrease in natural habitat. Fragmentation of habitat and soil degradation also play a role in the loss of certain species. Nowadays homogenization of specific species is resorted to, in the agricultural sector with the purpose of increasing production. But it has a negative result on biodiversity, as the ecosystem becomes dependent on fewer species, which in turn leads to extinction of some varieties and later on, a loss of traditional knowledge in the cultivation of indigenous species. A good example of habitat conversion was seen when six million hectares of humid forests was lost between 1990 and 1997. Deforestation trends differ between regions and countries. In tropical Asia, for instance 65% of the total forests have been destroyed: Bangladesh coming first with the highest rate of 96%, Sri Lanka with 86% and India coming close to 78%.

India is a country which is immensely rich in biodiversity with a 7-8% of the recorded species in the world: it stands at the seventh position in the world in mammal species, ninth in birds and fifth in reptiles. Its share of crops is 44% as compared to the world average of 11%. The country has 23.9% of its geographical area under forests and tree covers. Therefore biodiversity in India is important because it provides food from crops, livestock, forestry and fish. Industrial products such as timber, oils, lubricants, food flavours, industrial enzymes, cosmetic perfumes, dyes etc. can be derived from plant species. It is a source of economical wealth.

Human intervention is one of the chief reasons for ecological imbalance, habitat conversion, and as a result a loss of traditionally available Natural Resources, not to mention the extinction of potentially useful species. Habitat conversion has also lowered food production due to increased costs for agriculture, forestry, fisheries, water management and human health.

2. **Over exploitation**:

Development of a region or a country should address the ecological factor or else it will lead to 'Ecocide.' The practice of the global trend of 'invasive alien species competition' and 'predation on Native Species' has impacted ecosystems. As human beings increase in population, there is a corresponding increase in the exploitation on plant and animal species. Recent surveys have shown the increase in the depletion of large animals from many biological communities and so habitats have become 'empty.' In India, elephants and tigers are decreasing in number as result of the profit-motivate activities of human beings. The musk deer that was earlier spread throughout the Himalayan sub-alpine forests is now confined to a quarter of its former habitat range. This animal is killed for a special gland or musk pod found in the abdominal region of the male. Musk fetches 40,000 to 60,000 US $. About 2000 male deer have to be killed to obtain one kilogram of musk (Joshi and Joshi, 2004). An estimated amount of 1-3 million tonnes of wild meat is harvested annually from the Congo Basin. This is sometimes said to be six times the sustainable rate. Wild meat trade is a large but invisible contributor to the national economies dependent on the resource. Such practices, termed over exploitation of the species leads to spread of diseases from Animals to Humans to Climate Change.

Ramachandra Guha in his book *The Unquiet Woods* (1989), has explored the radical ecological change in the Himalayan regions during the British rule. Guha (2000) mentions the excessive cutting of *banj* oak and other broad- leaved trees by the Britishers in the mid-nineteenth century to build railway tracks and sleeper-coach berths. He argues that large scale deforestation, followed by the steady introduction of timber monocultures has brought a dramatic ecological rupture in the Himalayan region. In another book titled, *This Fissured Land* (Gadgil and Guha, 1992), based on a study of the ecology in South Asia, and gives some insights on the history of ecology in this region. The Himalaya region had a predominance of self-sufficient communities such as hunter gatherers, nomads, and subsistence agriculturists. These were 'ecosystem people' who crafted a range of subsistence livelihood through the prudent use of natural resources (Gadgil and Guha, 1992:113). "Human history is as a whole, precisely such a patchwork of prudence and profligacy, of sustainable and exhaustive resource use" (3).The colonial-ecological-watershed (CEW) framework of Guha and Gadgil, though written to provide a historical context to the destructive impacts brought by British rule in India, also serve as a pointed critique of the intensification of environment degradation in post independent India.

3. Global Warming

This causes ecosystems to shift northward or upward in altitude. Even a one degree change in temperature corresponds to hundred kilometers change in latitude. The average shift in habitat condition by the year 2100 is estimated to be 140 to 580 kilometers. Higher temperatures cause early flowering and this can affect interactions with other species which are dependent on flowering plants. Climate change is affecting species which have already been impacted by multiple threats such as habitat fragmentation due to colonization, logging, agriculture, mining etc. All these contribute to the further destruction of terrestrial habitats.

Coral reef mortality has increased and erosion has accelerated due to increasing temperatures. In 1998, 16% of the world's corals died due to this. To add to this the increase in the levels of carbon dioxide in the atmosphere, adversely impacts the coral building process called 'calcification.' Scientists estimate calcification to decline significantly in the coming years.

Sea levels rise due to global warming which will lead to the disappearance of low-lying areas in the world and extinction of island species. In equatorial regions, growth of plants will be disturbed. Many species which are sensitive to rapid climate change will become extinct. Another major impact of global warming will be manifested in temperate regions as it will go greener as a result of increased plant growth. This will follow a resultant decrease in biodiversity and vegetation in the equatorial regions. Global climate change affects the food cycle changes at local and global levels. The present trend of increasing popularity of Asian and Arabic food in temperate countries is an indication of a paradigmatic shift in the food habits of people there. Conversely the trend of Western cuisine by Indians in Cosmopolitan cities will also lead to multiple changes in the cultivation of biodiversity, habitat conversion, and agriculture.

4. **Natural Calamities.**

Natural calamities such as floods, cyclones, landslides, earthquakes etc. are also responsible for depletion of biological biodiversity. For instance, during the monsoon of 1998 the entire Kaziranga National Park in Assam was heavily flooded. It resulted in the death of 28 rhinos, between 70 to 80 deer, 8 bears and 3 elephants, besides many plant species that were lost forever.

The flood in the coastal areas of Kerala in 2018 is said to have claimed the lives of about 1000 people, in addition to major damage to the infrastructure, economy and livestock. India is a country which is vulnerable to floods as it has 45.64 million hectares of flood-prone land out of its total geographical area of 329 million hectares. The total number of lives lost in the last 64 years, due to floods is 107,487.

5. **Energy Resources**.

Development and utilization of various forms of energy resources such as fossil fuel (crude oil, coal, and natural gas), biomass energy, nuclear energy, hydroelectricity and other non-conventional energy sources have direct implications on biodiversity. Development of these energy sources modifies natural habitat and alters the evolutionary process. Development and utilization of fossil fuels accelerates global climatic change and associated disturbances, such as air pollution, and these when combined with the increase of human population will eventually cause severe loss of biodiversity.

Development of biomass requires vast stretches of land to be under agriculture. This results in conversion of natural landscapes into agricultural land. It also leads to monoculture and destroys the biodiversity of the region. Development of hydroelectricity power necessitates water storage in highlands, due to which large areas under forest and grasslands submerge under water. The Narmada Bachao Andolan led by Medha Patker was precisely about the government's negligence in the rehabilitation of 3000 villagers whose houses and farms had been submerged in the Sardar Sarovar Hydro-electric project.

Resistance as strategy

There have been a number of different forms of resistance by peasants and villagers to protest against environment exploitation. Environmental movements favour sustainable management of natural resources and invites governmental intervention wherever possible to solve the issue. In her article on the subject, Priyanka Sunil has mentioned seven movements in India that were resistance strategies of the local people against environmental issues that would disturb the ecological balance of the territory and cause biodiversity losses.

1. Bishnoi Movement: It took place in the 1700s in a village named Khejarli, in Marwar region of Rajasthan. The Bishnoi[2] villagers in Khejarli and

surrounding villages resisted the felling of sacred trees. Amrita Devi, a villager spearheaded the resistance by hugging the tree when the contractors came with workers to cut it down. She encouraged others to do the same. It is believed, that 363 Bishnoi villagers were killed in this protest demonstration. When the King came to know of this, he is said to have rushed to the village and apologized. After that he declared the Bishnoi state as a protected area. The legislation regarding this still exists in the region.

2. Chipko Movement: It started in the hilly district of Tehri-Gharwal, of Uttarakhand state in the Himalayan region in 1973. This was also a resistance by the locals against deforestation in the region. It was led by Sundarlal Bhaguna, a villager, who set out to educate the villagers about the importance of trees in checking soil erosion, cause rains and to purify the air. The women of Advani village of Tehri-Garhwal tied sacred threads around the tree trunks and hugged it. Hence the protest came to be called 'Chipko' movement. The movement gathered momentum in 1978 and the women faced police firings and tortures. The Chief Minister at that time, set up a committee and it reported in favour of the villagers. This movement became a turning-point in the history of eco-development struggles, regionally, nationally and globally.

3. Save Silent Valley Movement: It happened in 1978. Silent Valley is an evergreen tropical forest in Palakkad district of Kerala. It came into news when several NGOs opposed the construction of a hydroelectric dam across river Kunthipuzha, which runs through Silent Valley. The Planning Commission of India approved the project in February 1973, at a cost of about 25 crores. Following a concerted effort by a number of NGOs

and the public criticism concerning the project, in January 1981, the then Prime Minister Indira Gandhi was forced to revise this decision and declare the Silent Valley a protected area. In 1985, Prime Minister, Rajiv Gandhi, inaugurated the Silent Valley National Park.

4. Jungle Bachao Andolan: The agitation was started in Singhbhum district of Bihar. The tribals of the area, protested against the government's decision to replace natural forests with the planting of highly-priced teak trees. Later this movement spread to Jharkhand and Orissa.

5. Appiko Movement: It was a stir by the local people of Uttara Kannada and Shimoga districts of Karnataka. It was considered the southern version of the Northern Chipko Movement. The movement was called 'Appiko Chaluvali. 'The mode of protest was the same as in the earlier movement: the locals embraced the trees which were going to be cut down by the forest department contractors. The second phase of the movement focused on afforestation on denuded lands. Later on, the movement focused on the rational use of ecosphere by introducing alternative energy resource to reduce pressure on the forests. The movement became a huge success.

6. Narmada Bachao Andolan: This was an agitation led by environmentalist and activist Medha Patker to demand rehabilitation to the villagers who had lost their homes and property in the Sardar Sarovar Dam Project. Later on the movement turned its focus to the preservation of the environment and the preservation of the valley.

The role of politics in shaping ecology is greater today than it has been in the past. This is due to the rapid social and technological changes that have impacted the 'natural environment' (MaKibbens, 1989). Political ecology studies power struggles in environment resources, management and conservation. In 2012, Anthony Bebbington published a lecture titled "Underground Political Ecologies" which demanded more focus on extractive sectors (Bebbington, 2012). Academic works that focus on the interface between politics and environmental degradation has often been labelled 'political ecology' (Blaike, 1985). It exposes the politics behind dispossession and conservation strategies employed.

The neo-Marxist basis of Third World political ecology explained local environmental conflicts in terms of class relations and surplus extraction linked to global capitalist production (Cliffe, and Hedlund, 1979; O'Brien, 1985). The state was often typically seen as being little more than an agent of capital, thereby obscuring both the potential autonomy of this actor vis-à-vis capital, and the diversity of bureaucratic interest which the state often encompass. Concerns over the influence of deterministic neo-Marxism on the fields of development led in the late 1980s to a second phase of political ecology, which was drawn on a more eclectic range of theoretical sources. Blaike and Brookefield (1987), Hecht and Cockburn (1989) and Guha (1989) initiated this process with their study on land degradation, the Amazon and India. It was followed by a flood of research along similar lines. All this sought to demonstrate a more complex understanding of how power relations mediate human-environmental interaction than hitherto was the case.

The potential power of grass root actors, such as poor farmers and shifting cultivators in environmental conflicts has been emphasized with reference to the concepts of avoidance behaviour and everyday resistance as part of an attempt to link political ecology to developments in social movements theorizing (Guha, 1989; Peluso, 1992). Scholars who focused on household studies (Guyer and Peters, 1987; Berry, 1989) as well as ecofeminists, have examined how power relations within the household influence the control of land, natural resources, labour, and capital (Carney, 1993; Schroeder, 1993). Recent studies upon 'post structuralism' and 'discourse theory' (Said, 1978; Bhabha, 1994; Escobar, 1995) show how knowledge and power interrelate so as to mediate political-ecological outcomes (Fairhead and Leach, 1995; Peet and Watts, 1996).

The Third World is today facing environmental crisis over problems such as tropical deforestation, soil erosion or desertification. These environmental problems cannot be understood in isolation from the political and economic contexts within which they exist. Harvey says that "all ecological projects (and arguments) are simultaneously political-economic projects (and arguments) and vice versa." The First World states tend to favour the view that many of the environmental problems in the Third World is due to the 'runaway' population growth which contributes simultaneously to social poverty and environmental degradation. However, as the perceived link between tropical deforestation and global warming illustrates, the Third World's problems are now the world's problems. This situation is being used by the First World to justify the growing interference through bilateral and multilateral mechanisms in Third World social and environment matters (Sachs,1993; Miller,1995). In contrast many Third World states emphasize the contribution of the First World States towards these problems.

Third World Political Ecology (1997) by Raymond L. Bryant and Sinead Bailey provides an insight into the research that aims to develop an integrated understanding of the political economy and the environmental change in the Third World. Since the 1980s the political ecology in the Third World is engaging the attention of researchers of environmental studies. New insights have emerged about the ways environment is politicized and how in this 'political environment' the roles of various actors: states, multilateral institutions, businesses, environmental non-governmental organizations, poverty –stricken groups play a part. A good example of this is manifested in the policies and practices of the FAO (Food and Agriculture Organization).

The technical organization (FAO) was established by the United Nations in 1945, to promote rational agriculture, forestry, fisheries policies in member states. This was primarily to "develop world agriculture, to enable the world to feed itself" (Sesmon, 1991:47). In view of this a series of measures were adopted to 'modernize' the agricultural sector, promote the export of cash crops and enhance productivity as well as efficiency. Though the role of the FAO was indirect and revolved around providing technical advice and support to states, and agencies for planning agricultural development, it has been evident that the FAO has always linked itself with colonial states. As a result the FAO worked with the view that the natural resource management strategies of grass root actors throughout the Third World were 'backward' and 'inefficient' (Richard, 1985).

As in colonial times, 'progress' for the FAO meant increased production for the market, as well as modernization in methods of production. In an important policy document first published in 1979 (World Agriculture: Towards 2000), the FAO remained adamant about the modernization of agriculture (Sesmou, 1991). In the late 1980s, the FAO insisted that if Africa did not employ modern agricultural methods, it could seriously affect the sector. In the fisheries sector, meanwhile the emphasis was on increasing the capacity of fishers in order to increase catches through more technologically 'sophisticated' fishing vessels (Fairlie, 1995). The concern in the forestry sector was largely to promote commercial forest plantations so as to meet the rapidly increasing demand in the world for timber. In each of these cases, the outcome has been to deepen the environmental degradation and the social marginalization of poor grass root actors. The politics in ecology is rampant, leading to fierce conflicts between environmentalists and agriculturists and between state and society. Local traditional knowledge was dismissed by FAO as inferior to 'modern' western knowledge systems. This conflict is simultaneously a battle for control over environmental resources and a struggle over ideas concerning the best way to use and manage these resources.

Women and Ecology

In the 1970s, peasant women from the region in Garhwal Himalaya, came out in defense of the forests. The Chipko Movement was one of its kind in educating Indians about biodiversity and biodiversity-based living economies. Shiva boldly states in her book *Monocultures of the Mind* (1993) that the failure to understand biodiversity and its many functions, is at the root of the impoverishment of nature and culture. Shiva applied the lessons she had learned about diversity in the Himalayan forests to the protection of biodiversity on her farms. At first, she started saving seeds from farmers' fields and then realized that she needed a farm for demonstration and training. Thus, Navdanya Farm[3] was started in 1994 in the Doon Valley, located in the lower elevation Himalayan region of Uttarakhand Province. The well-known environmentalist who comes from the same region, Vandana Shiva, states that her involvement in contemporary ecology movement began with Chipko Movement which was a non-violent response to the large-scale deforestation that was taking place in the Himalayan region. Logging had led to landslides and floods, which when combined with a scarcity of water, fodder, and fuel made the life of women unbearable; for, since women provided these basic needs, the scarcity meant longer walks for collecting water and firewood, and a heavier burden. The

Garhwal women knew that the real value of forests was not the timber from a dead tree, but the springs and streams, food for their cattle, and fuel for their hearths.

The privatization of land for revenue displaced women more critically, eroding their traditional land rights. The expansion of cash crops undermined food production and women were often left with meagre resources to feed and care for their children, the aged and infirm in situations where their men had migrated or were conscripted into forced labour by the colonizers. The displacement of women from the economy destroyed woman's productivity both by removing land, water, and forests from their management and control, as well as through ecological destruction of soil, water, and vegetation systems in such a way that nature's productivity and renewability were impaired. While gender subordination and patriarchy are the oldest of oppressions, they have taken on new and more violent forms through the project of development.

Women and the Environment was one of the critical areas of concern identified at the Beijing Platform for Actions in 1995. The Conference made linkages between poverty, natural disasters, health problems, unsustainable development and gender inequalities. Today women struggle against global trends, but they are working together to affect change. By establishing domestic and non-governmental organizations, many women have recognized themselves and acknowledged to the world that they have the right to participate in environmental dilemmas; notwithstanding the fact that they have a different relationship with nature than the men: different needs, responsibilities and knowledge about natural resources. Issues such as environmental degradation, pollution, deforestation, and overpopulation impact women in a different way. Women are often the most directly affected by environmental issues, hence they become more concerned about environmental problems. According to United Nations Chronicle   there is a link between breast cancer and the pesticide DDT.

Women's role in the environment domain has always been significant. However, society has systematically excluded her interactions over the ages. Most of the historical books have been advocating the role of the participation of men in environmental activities and have ignored the participation of women. Consequently the role of women in environmental issues have been hidden from history. However, the twenty first century is witnessing phenomenal changes in the role and activity of women in environmental issues. Ecofeminism, a new discipline that emerged in the 1970s works on the premise that there is a connection between women and environment in terms of vulnerability, exploitation by powerful groups, and the treatment meted out to both. Ecofeminists see ecological degradation and women's oppression as two sides of the same coin. The proponents of Ecofeminism foster resistance to formations of domination for the sake of human liberation and planetary survival.

Women and Environmental Empowerment

Women form the largest group of the world's poorest and vulnerable people. They are represented in a disproportionate manner and are often on the front lines of the climate change. In developing countries in particular, due to their role as primary providers of food, water, and fuel for their families, women are not only the most affected by climate change but are also a pivotal force for building responses to direct climate impacts. . More importantly, women are frequently the decision makers about household consumption. They represent an increasing share of wealth around the world, yet they are not included or allowed to participate in decision ma0ing roles in climate change bodies at the national and international levels. The fundamental explanation for the lack of gender considerations in climate debates, generally, is the fact that women are poorly represented in planning and decision-making processes thus limiting their capacity to engage in political decisions related to climate change. At the national level the picture is similar. The integration of women is most likely to succeed at the re gional and local levels, but even here, it is the exception rather than the rule.

Generally women's involvement with nature has been ignored. Most of the historical books have been advocating the role and participation of men in environmental activities; while the contribution made by women on the land and in the household have remained hidden, ignored or undocumented. She is also familiar with the forest from where she gets firewood for the home and fodder for her livestock. Yet society and its policy-makers have strived to exclude her from debates and strategies connected with forestry. Their voices and their wisdom have often been retained only through Oral literature and songs that have been passed on to successive generations.

The Centre for Indigenous Knowledge Systems in India noted that in a study of two villages in Tamil Nadu, women have intimate knowledge and understanding of the traditional rice varieties as well as their preparation. This is also the case with vegetables and seeds (Vijaylakshmi, 1998). In Rwanda women produce more than 600 varieties of beans (Howard, 2003). In Bangladesh women always preserve and conserve seeds. In the rural households there is a practice of sharing seeds among sisters, neighbours, and relatives enhance the biodiversity and genetic resources. Consequently, families have a larger variety of food, some of which would even be unavailable in the local market (Akhter, 2001).

The well-known environmentalist and activist Vandana Shiva upholds women's knowledge in agriculture especially in the storage and preparation of seed for the sowing. She argues that it involves visual discrimination of the good seeds from the bad ones: a skill and an expertise that comes from experience in agriculture (Shiva, 1991). In most places in India it is the women who do the sowing and the reaping. All this requires knowledge of the weather conditions together with traditional skills of agriculture. Although mechanization in agriculture has nowadays limited the involvement of women considerably in the harvesting and winnowing activities, women are still employed for the rest of the processes, including sowing and storing of grain. Since women are naturally nurturers and caregivers in the household, it is only natural that she will take upon herself the responsibility of sustaining the life of her family through the food she grows and cooks. What is labour to the man, is more of a duty and a responsibility for the women. She is happy to be involved in this way as it satisfies her maternal instincts: she is a 'mother' a 'giver' just like earth. Therefore, the role of women in the use of natural resources and biodiversity is significant, because they are nurturers who sustain the livelihood of the family through food. "Even though the rural women are relatively poor and uneducated, they are the chief sustainers of rural microeconomics activities" (Gupta U. C. et.al. 856). Women's knowledge in agriculture, biodiversity, sustainable development, and nature conservation can prove to be invaluable to traditional knowledge and practices of the region.

Women as conservers of biodiversity

In Pakistan, KHOJ, Research and Publication Centre, documented the traditional cultural practices in two villages. In the reports, it was mentioned that women of the villages use weeds as source of food for human and animal consumption. Greens like 'Baathu' that grew with the wheat in the fields were plucked and cooked in a 'greens' preparation that is considered a delicacy. The same plant is also used in Yunaani and Ayurveda medical treatments for curing stomach ailments. Wild plants are often the main source of food for indigenous communities everywhere in the world. The conservation of this often the domain of the women of the region. For instance, women in Kenya and Bangladesh use biodiversity to conserve food for the rainy season when water logging prevents the availability of fresh food from the fields. Samoan women healers use 100 different plant species for treatments of various maladies. The indigenous women of Madhya Pradesh in India, use a combination of plants as contraceptives (Cox, 1995; Cox, 2000; CSE 1982).

There are a number of women who manage vegetable gardens for their home consumption as well as for income. While the rural women have always cultivated plants in the spaces around their habitation, nowadays the urban woman has taken to it in a big way, partly as a hobby and partly for consumption of good organic vegetables. There are regions where women cultivate their own gardens that contain high levels of diversity. These are models of sustainable land use (Huvio, 1999).

In a research conducted Soumi Kundu, by a scholar from the Centre for Development Research, Pune, on the status of kitchen gardens, it was discovered that 600 households in Jharkhand had benefited through enriched diets procured from kitchen gardens. An initial survey conducted by Public Health Foundation of India (PHFI) showed that females of Gumla district between the age of 16 and 22 suffered from severe anaemia. This was a district that had 71% of tribal households and 65% made their living through cultivation. The farmers here grew pulses, vegetables, and other crops. However due to their poverty the farmers were forced to sell all their produce for livelihood, while they survived on a watery gruel of rice or any of the pulses they had kept aside. Even such a meal was available only once daily. When natural calamities strike, they do not even have a one-time meal; they are forced to sustain themselves and their families on water. In order to enrich the villagers' diet kitchen gardens were seen as an option. An NGO named PRADAN (Professional Assistance for Development) piloted by Poshan Vari in July 2016, promoted nutrition-based cultivation models in homestead lands. Available spaces near the house were used. Poshan Vari gardens were grown in 47 villages across nine panchayats. About 600 households participated in this venture.[4] This NGO provides a rich blend of seeds, local varieties of cereals, pulses, green leafy vegetables and these are organically grown by the women. Kitchen Garden model has helped to improve the health of women in Gumla district. It has helped to fix the skewed gender pattern in food consumption prevalent in Gumla and across India.

A study conducted in Nigeria found that women who cultivate intensive home gardens may grow 18 to 57 plant species, including tubers, legumes, grains, and fruit trees in addition to raising poultry (Huvio, 1999). According to Patricia Howard women provide 79% of total vegetable food (Howard, 2003). Howard goes on to say that women's local knowledge is complex, holistic, innovative, and responds to external and internal change. Women have a multifaceted role: as plant gatherers, home gardeners, herbalists, and seed custodians.

Local knowledge: Holistic and Sustainable

Rituals and symbolic ceremonies are important elements in Third World countries because poverty and hardship drive human beings to seek comfort and solace in religion. The religion of the communities demand prayer rituals which often use specific flowers/plant/ fruit/ vegetables for the occasion. In many places it is women who cultivate and take care of the supply of such flowers etc. for sacred rituals.

Women as well as men have kept the observance of religious practices down the ages. Traditional farming communities have a deeper understanding of nature as well as the relationship of mankind with nature. This belief in the oneness of Creation (humans-plants-animals-cosmos) is a deep-seated belief of many rural indigenous communities all over the world. For instance, in India "Negilu Pooja" is conducted in some areas, before the sowing of the seed. There is also a practice where the womenfolk evoke the forces essential for a good crop before the seeds are stored for the next sowing. (Ramprasad, 1999). In the Philippines, there are practices and rituals followed by indigenous communities at every stage of the planting of rice and other crops. Such kinds of practices are holistic as it encompasses the spiritual, human and natural world continue to be of major importance for farmers and cultivators both in the rural and urban world. (Haverkort and Heimstra, 1999). Western imperialism destroyed the practice of customs and beliefs of indigenous communities in the colonies of Asia, Africa, Latin America and other smaller islands populated by indigenous communities; a lot of their traditional knowledge and cultural practices were lost with the onset of political colonization.

The holistic concept has been lacking in Western thinking. In fact, during the middle Ages, in Europe, there existed women healers who used herbs and prayers for healing and they were branded as witches and burnt as heretics. Ceremonies and rituals that were part of the rural landscape were also branded as witchcraft.

The spread of Christianity in these non-western countries also contributed in a way to the loss of traditional customs surrounding agriculture (Hecht,1995) Many of the scientists in the western world looked down upon traditional knowledge as unscientific and without rational basis. Therefore it came to be replaced by mechanized and technologically- advanced methods of agriculture. To equate traditional knowledge as superstition and to condemn the indigenous beliefs and practices of these communities was a fall out of colonization and it has had a far-reaching effect upon the present attitude of the people towards in the environment. Local paradigms were changed for colonial/western paradigms, industrialization introduced new methods everywhere.

PAN AP (Pesticide Action Network, Asia and Pacific) has initiated and collaborated with network partners from India (CIKS), Pakistan (KHOJ) and Indonesia to pilot a study on the projection of women's knowledge in sustainable agriculture. SIBAT from Philippines has also joined in this collaboration. A series of workshops were organized by PAN AP in Penang between 1998 and 2000 to discuss the concept and framework for the pilot study, methodology for the data collection, compilation and utilization of the data in the reports. Such initiatives will prove helpful in the future for sustainable agriculture systems. Women farmers with their knowledge systems and innovation have a lot to contribute. Food security and sovereignty must begin with women farmers and be built on their knowledge and experience. Formal scientific systems have to nurture and work with farmers in complementary, equitable and non-exploitative collaboration in order to take up the challenge of achieving global food security and sovereignty.

Conclusion

Anthropocene, a distinct intellectual rubric for exploring human challenges and prospects in an already climate changed world, claims to offer new conceptual grounds for radically re-visioning the existing challenges that confront humanity. Instead of the earlier anxieties of an overpopulated planet running out of resources. The Anthropocene warns of a crisis brought on by tipping points from excess GreenHouse Gas (GHG) emissions, climate chaos from a heated planet and the crossing of critical bio-physical thresholds. The Anthropocene eco-catastrophe, hence, is less about the struggle over resource scarcities, than it is about sustaining conditions for planetary life. The pursuit for development at the cost of ecological imbalances, especially from the 1950s onwards bear striking continuities with colonial environmental legacies in which nature has been transformed into a profitable commodity that earns profits. Instead of taking strategies designed by western environment researchers blindly, countries in Asia, Africa, South Pacific regions would be wise to include local knowledge, and active women participation for future paradigms that will conserve nature in its resources and biodiversity. The UN dialogue on Harmony with Nature (2018) has emphasized the need for production and consumption systems based on principles of reciprocity, returning fertility to the soil and helping to ensure the health of non-human elements of nature. Recent trends show that worldwide here is a growing commitment to protecting nature with the adoption of new legislations that grant rights to natural entities.

Endnote

1. "Earth jurisprudence" refers to a philosophy of law and human governance in which humans are only one part of a wider community of beings and the well-being of each member of that community is dependent on the well-being of the Earth as a whole.
2. The Navdanya Farm under the guidance of Vandana Shiva, conserves and grows 630 varieties of rice, 150 varieties of wheat, and hundreds of other species.

Shiva and her team practice and promote a biodiversity-intensive form of farming that produces more food and nutrition per acre proving the fact that the conservation of biodiversity is, therefore, also the answer to the food and nutrition crisis. This pioneering effort in organic farming which started way back in the late 1980's has shown the way for biodiversity conservation. So far, the team has worked with farmers to set up more than 100 community seed banks across India. They have saved more than 3,000 rice varieties as well as helped farmers make a transition from fossil fuel and chemical-based monocultures to biodiverse ecological systems nourished by the sun and the soil. planet running out of resources,

3. They were called Bishnoi because they followed the teachings of Guru Maharaj Sambiji who was the founder of the Bishnoi faith in 1485.The religion did not approve of any harm to be done upon trees and animals.

4. Poshan Vari-A follow up survey conducted by Centre for Development Research, Pune, reported that households in Gumla were able to save 1600 to 3200 rupees in a month with about 60 to 90 hours of labour in their kitchen gardens. In addition to this, kitchen gardens helped to improve the diet of the villagers significantly. Poshan Vari sees women as key participants in growing kitchen gardens.

Bibliography

Akhter, F. *Seeds in Women's Hands:A symbol of food security and solidarity.* New Delhi: Sage publications, 2001. print.

Bebbington, A., Carrasco, H., Peralbo, L.,Ramon, G., Torres, V.H., and Truijilli,J. "Fragile Lands, fragile organizations: Indian organizationsand the politics of sustainability in Ecuador." *Transactions of the Institute of British Geographers, 18.* (1993): 179-96. Print.

Berkes, F. (Ed). *Common Property Resources: Ecology and Community Based Sustainable Development.* London: Belhaven, 1989. Print.

Bhabha, H.K. *The Location of Culture.* London: Routledge, 1994. Print.

Blaike, P. *The Political Economy of Soil Erosion.* London: Longman, 1985. Print.

Blaikie, P. and Brookfield, H. *Land Degradation and Society.* London: Methuen, 1987. Print.

Byrant, Raymond L. and Sinead Bailey. *Third World Political Ecology.* London: Routledge, 1997. Print.

Carney, J. "Converting the wetlands, engendering the environment: the intersection of gender and agrarian change in the Gambia. ." *Economic Geography 69* (1993): 329-48. Print.

Carson, R. *Silent Spring.* Boston: Houghton Mifflin, 1962. Print.

Cooper,D.Vellve,R and Hobbelink,H . *Genetic Resources and Local Food Security.* London: Intermediate Technology Publications, 1992. print.

Cox, P.A. "Shamin as Scientist: indigenous knowledge systemsin pharmacological research and conservation." Hostettman, K et.al. *Phytochemistry of plants used in traditional medicine.* Oxford: Clarendon Press, 1995. print.

—. "Will tribal knowledge survive the millennium?" *Science:287* (2000): 44-45. print.

Fairhead, J and Leach, M. "False forest history, complicit social analysis: rethinking some Western African environmental narration." *World Development 23* (1995): 1023-35. Print.

Gadgil, Madhav and Guha, Ramachandra. *This Fissured Land : An Ecological History of India.* Berkeley and Los Angeles: University of California Press, 1993. print.

Ghate, V.S. "Plants in patra-pooja: Notes on their identity and utilization." *Ethnobotany 10 (1-2)* (1998): 6-15. print.

Guha, Ramachandra. *The Unquiet Woods: Ecological Change and Peasant Resistance in the Himalaya.* Berkley, Los Angelos, California: University of California Press, 1989. print.

Guyer, J.L. and Peters, P.E (Eds). "Conceptualizing and household: issues of theory and policy in Africa." *Development and Change. Special Issue.* (1987). Print.

Halim, A AB, et al. "Indigenous Knowledge and Biodiversity Conservation in Sabah, Malaysia." *International Journal of Social Science and Humanity 2(2)* (2012): 159-163. print.

Haverkort, B and Hiemstra, W. *Food for Thought: Ancient visions and new experiments of rural people.* Netherlands, Bangalore, London: ETC/Compass, Books for Change and Zed Books, 1999. Print.

Hecht, S.B. *Agroecology:The Science of Sustainable Agriculture.* London & USA: West View Press and International Technology, 1995. Print.

Hedlund, H. "Contradiction in the periphalization of a pastoral society: the Maasai." *Review of African Political Economy 15/16* (1979): 53-62. Print.

Howard, P. "The Major Importance of 'Minor' Resources: Women and Plant Biodiversity." *Gatekeepers Series No.112.* London: International Institute for Environmentand Development, 2003. print.

Huvio, T. *Gender and Local Knowledge.* FAO report. Switzerland: FAO Women in Development Service, 1999. print.

Ingold, T. "Culture and the perception of the environment." Croll, E. and Parkin, D (Eds). *Bush Base, Forest Farm: Culture, Environment and Development.* London: Routledge, 1992. 39-56. Print.

Mckibbens, B. *The End of Nature.* New York: Viking, 1989. print.

Natarajan, B. *Biodiversity and Traditional Knowledge: Perspectives.* 28 June 2012. online. 28 June 2019.

O'Brien, J. "Sowing the seeds of famine: the political economy of food deficits in Sudan." *Review of African Political Economy,33* (1985): 23-32. print.

Peluso, N.L. *Rich Forests: Poor People: Resource Control and Resistance in Java.* Berkeley: University of California Press, 1992. Print.

Periera, W. *Tending the Earth: Traditional Sustainable Agriculture in India.* Bombay: Earthcare books, 1993. print.

Pitts, D.C. "Deforestation : Social Dynamics ." (Ed), D.C. Pitt. *Watersheds and Mountain Ecosystems.* London: RoutledgePrint, 1989. 132-58.

—. "Environment and access to resources in Africa. ." *Africa* (1989): 18-40. print.

Ramprasad, V. "Women and biodiversity Conversation." COMPAS, October 1999. print.

Said, E.W. *Orientalism*. Harmondsnorth: Penguin, 1978. Print.

Scott, A. *Ideology and the New Social Movements*. London: Unwin Hyman, 1990. print.

Scott, J.C. *The Moral Economy of the Peasant Resistance*. New Haven: Yale University Press, 1976. Print.

Shiva, V and Dankelman,I. "Women and Biological Diversity: Lessons from the Indian Himalaya." Cooper, R and Hobbelink,H et.al. *Growing Diversity: Genetic Resources and Local Food Security*. London: Intermediate Technology Publications, 1992. 44-50. print.

Shiva, V. "Monoculturs,Monoplies,Myths and the Masculinisationof Agriculture." *Women's Knowledge, Biotechnology and International Trade: Fostering a New Dialogue into the Millenium* . Washington, June 28- july 2. June -July 1998. print.

Sunil, Priyanka. *7 Major Environmental Movements in India*. june 2019. online.

Vijaylakshmi, K. *Documentation of Women's Knowledge in Sustainable Agriculture*. India: Pesticide Action Network and the Pacific and Centre for Indian Knowledge Systems, 1998. Print.

Watts, M. *Silent Violence: Food, Famine and Peasantry in Northern Nigeria*. Berkeley: University of California Press, 1983a. Print.

Reading Arab Women's Literature through Intersectionality

- B. V. Saraswathy

Bio: Dr. B. V. Saraswathy is an Assistant Professor, Department of English at C.T.T.E. College for Women, Chennai.

Abstract:
The Omani writer Jokha Alharthi has been awarded the Man Booker International Prize for 2019 for her novel *Celestial Bodies* translated by Marilyn Booth, who also shares the award. This paper aims to analyse the intersectionality of religion, societal traditions and patriarchy in the novel *Celestial Bodies*. The novel describes the changes in the country of Oman brought in by the discovery of petroleum resources. Alharthi beguilingly coalesces the history of the land with that of the people by interweaving the changes in the lives of three generations of characters that she presents in the novel. The women in the novel have

to fight against the combined triad of religion, tradition and patriarchy to preserve their individuality and carve an identity of their own. Portrayals of women in Arabic literature serve as a barometer by which the status and role of Arab women in society can be measured (Mona Mikhailis). The narration compiles the lives of the women pulling at the edges of rapid change in the country and is narrated alternatively by a character, Abdallah and the third person voice of the author. The bond between the grandmother, daughter and granddaughter are brought out from the intense private sphere of family life in which the Arab world has placed it and "the great unwritten story" of the "cathexis between mother and daughter" that is "essential, distorted, misused" (Adrienne Rich) is presented with finesse and sensitivity with an underlying urgency and passion. The paper aims to demonstrate how an intersectional reading of the novel reveals the gender dynamics and social change in Oman and the importance of this novel as a palimpsest.

Keywords: Arab women's novels, Omani women, gender, patriarchy.

The term 'Intersectionality' was coined by Kimberlé Crenshaw and it "emerged in the late 1980s as an analytic frame capable of attending to the particular positionality of black women and other women of color" (Cooper 385). Crenshaw argues that the problems of black women were set against a 'single axis' whereas they should be considered against the backdrop of "multidimensionality of Black women's experiences" (385) and that they should not be included within an already established analytical structure. Crenshaw sees 'intersectionality' as 'structural intersectionality' (where the three systems of power, i.e. race, gender and class domination, converge) and 'political intersectionality' (where women of colour are situated within at least two subordinated groups that pursue conflicting political agenda).

Intersectionality thus "encapsulated and expanded to a body of work about a set of social problems" (389) and advanced the idea that systems of power became the systems of oppression under which women of colour lived. It focuses on the social and institutional practices that shape the experiences and lives of marginalised women and is recognised as "one of the most useful and expansive paradigms" (405) for thinking about operations of power. For the analysis of the relationship between the dominant, privileged, hegemonic sides of societal structural categories and their antithesis, intersectionality is an apt tool. Applying this tool to study the situation of the women of the Arabian countries, a fourth system of power - Religion - should also be considered in conjunction with race, gender and class. This paper aims to analyse the intersectionality of religion, societal traditions and patriarchy in the novel *Celestial Bodies*. The prominent role of religion is evident when it is used to institutionalise and perpetuate patriarchy.

In Arab culture, women had a low status for centuries. Economic development and state expansion are two major sources of social change in the Gulf countries since World War II and has effected a change in the social stratification and concomitantly the position of women in the new modernised society. While the influx of wealth from the discovery of oil in the region has created a materialistic society, the loyalties to Islam, and family and tribe, is supported by the state. Yvonne Yazbeck Haddad explains that "Islam became an integral part of tribal society" and the prevalent "tribal customs became a sacred tradition passed down from their ancestors" (149) which in praxis, counteracted the tenets of the Quran regarding the autonomy of a woman. Ever since the Western influence and processes of modernisation planted the seeds, feminist ideas began to germinate and the voice of the women protesting their lack of rights is becoming more and more strident. Arab women writers began feminist discourses about education, work and marriage. They examine the ways in which the power structures dictated the framework of their lives. In Mona Fayad's perception:

> ... one of the most difficult tasks confronting Arab women writers in inscribing themselves as subjects lies in resisting and renegotiating their role within a master national narrative that not only homogenizes the concept of national identity itself, but also assigns Woman a fixed role as a historical metaphor buried deep within the foundations of the narrative. Through this historical metaphor, Woman is appropriated as signifier of traditionalism, reservoir of a communal identity .... (147)

Rifat Hassan discusses feminism in Islam and the sources of the Islamic tradition and points out that women are considered "derivative creatures who can never be considered equal to men" (256). Hassan exhorts Muslim women to challenge the male-centered and male-controlled Muslim societies to acknowledge the egalitarianism evident in the Qur'anic statements about human creation. Hassan asserts that: "the Qur'an, which *is* the primary source on which Islam is founded, consistently affirms women's equality with men and their fundamental right to actualize the human potential that they possess equally with men" (275). Early nineteenth century saw the gathering momentum of the modern women's movement in the Arab world as a result of increased contact with the West. The Arab intellectuals and women activists debated the question of whether Islam itself required the practices of veiling and denying education to women or if the patriarchal system had imposed the restrictions on pseudo-religious grounds (Zeidan). When writings were produced the works imitated the norms established by the existing male-dominated literary tradition. In the genre of poetry, Arab women writers began to develop a distinct aesthetic as they developed more political awareness of themselves as women. The women began to subvert the system that denied them education and literary society, by establishing salons and journals of their own and managed to bring them into mainstream literary criticism and discussion.

Many educated women writers arrived on the scene and began writing about their own lives in the first–person narration signifying their break away from the established literary tradition of the previous generation (Zeidan). "Key themes were individualism, the drive to assert a personal and distinctly female identity, and demands for the social, sexual and political rights of women" (6).

Official education for girls was initiated in Oman in 1970 and therefore not much of written literature in English appears until the second half of the twentieth century, specifically in the 1980s. Yusuf al-Sharuni declares that "1983 is the year the Omani short story of all kinds was born [before that there was only] an embryo taking shape in the womb of the awakening" (Qtd. Ashour et al 281). Considering the genres in women's literature in the Arab peninsula, poetry seems to have been given more importance than novel, with drama falling far behind, although some importance has been given to children's literature and reaches the reading public through newspapers and magazines. Writers like Badriya al-Shihhi, Tiba Bint 'Abd Allah al-Kindi, 'A'isha Bint 'Ali ibn Sa'id al-Ni'mi, Zakiya Bint Salim al-'Ilwi, Safiya Bint Muhammad Sa'id al-Harithi, and Turkiya al-Busa'idi are referred to by Su'ad al-Mana in the chapter "The Arabian Peninsula and the Gulf" in which the author discusses the important writers of the area up to the year 1999 (Ashour et al 271). Al-Mana also mentions that in 1998, Khawla al-Zahiri published her collection, *Saba'* (Sheba), won a prize from the Girls' Clubs in Sharjah. Jokha Alharthi is an Omani writer whose novel in Arabic, *Sayyidat al-Qamar* was shortlisted for Zayed Award 2011. It has been translated into English by Marilyn

Booth and published in 2018 under the title *Celestial Bodies* which won the Man Booker International Prize 2019. The country of Oman is rich in oil, but poor in other resources, and its economy depends on industries that are not conducive for female employment as they are mainly capital oriented and not labour intensive. According to Haddad, the Quran guarantees the right of a woman to gainful employment. However, the denial of the right to exercise this freedom by family members, should be blamed on tradition, she opines.

The novel *Celestial Bodies* is set in a small town called al-Awafi and is woven around women characters, although there is a male voice that narrates in alternation with the third person point of view of the author. There are three sisters whose marriages are at the centre of the novel. The eldest is Mayya who has fallen in love with an empty handed scholar recently returned from London. She burns for him with her soul: "Mayya fixed all her thoughts on her beloved's spirit. She mustered every atom in her being and sent the lot marching into his. Then she held her breath. ... She sent her spirit into the ether, detaching herself completely from the world (CB 5).

However, a marriage with Abdallah, the narrator, is arranged by her parents. She docilely succumbs to the arrangement and remains a good wife. Her devotion, however, is towards her children rather than the husband who dotes on her. To his direct question "Do you love me?', she evades a direct answer and ripostes with: 'Where did you pick up these TV-show words? ... have they eaten up your mind?' (11). Mayya's acceptance of the marriage is the dictates of tradition.

In defiance of society, Mayya names her first born daughter, London. Everyone around her is nonplussed at the unusual appellation. Only she knows that it is a paean to her lost love, the unsuccessful scholar who had returned from London. Later when London is a Physician in Muscat and wants to marry another doctor whose parents had been slaves in the family of her mother and grandmother, Mayya renounces her daughter. Mayya locks London in a room and breaks her mobile phone to sever contact with the son of a slave. As much as Mayya is aware of the changes happening in society and the world and even though she has seen to it that her daughter has education, and every luxury in life that money could buy, it is not possible for Mayya to give up on the ideas and practices that have been followed for generations.

The second sister, Asma, reads the books that she rescued from the damp in the locked rooms of the house and aspired to be a 'bluestocking', a genteel young woman who has acquired knowledge of the world from reading books, without having the benefit of a formal education. The ideas that classical Arabic love poetry inspire in her are tested severely in her life when she is married to a man who finds his freedom only when he paints horses. Khalid, Asma's husband, had chosen her because he envisaged that she would "fall instantly into the orbit he had marked out, who would always be there but would also always stay just outside, yet without wanting to create her own celestial sphere, her own orbit" (194). This patriarchal attitude towards his wife and marriage does not intimidate Asma. Khalid's exuberant love and his intense withdrawal when the artistic mood possessed him, teaches 'Asma to accommodate to the situation' (196). Asma cultivates her own circle of friends, she pursues her education and acquires a job, she has also collected a number of books and she has 'formed her own celestial orbit' (196). The couple learn that they could orbit freely without colliding with each other, by creating enough space within the marriage. Domestic space is reclaimed by Asma when she understands that her husband is an artist who has to indulge in his flights of fancy to be able to create his art. Asma manages to establish an orbit above the confluence of patriarchy, gender and religion.

Khawla, the youngest sister refuses the alliance proposed by her parents and waits for her cousin to return from Canada, who eventually arrives, marries and leaves. Nasir had been her playmate when they were children and had marked her as his wife when another cousin tried to win her favour. He proclaimed that Khawla was his 'wife'. On this declaration is based Khawla's faith in Khalid, as she waits for him to return from Canada. Nasir's mother sponsors his trip and his stay in Canada. On her death, the money stops flowing and he is forced to return. Propitiously, his marriage with Khawla reopens his route to Canada. He had already set up a home with his Canadian girlfriend to whom he now returns and visits his wife and growing number of children for ten years, after which his girlfriend kicks him out which forces him to return home permanently.

Khawla, who has waited for four years to marry Nasir, and a further ten years for him to return home for good and settle down with his family, reclaims her domestic space by asking for a divorce. She had steered her life with him in mind after both her sisters had been married and waited for him with unflagging confidence in his return. She preserved her beauty and looks for her husband who had already married a foreigner. However, after the children are grown up and Nasir has settled down in his native country, Khawla feels that her identity has to be reclaimed. Now, Khawla is not willing to subjugate herself anymore: "She couldn't bear the past any longer" (239). She bears the responsibility of her decision to marry only Nasir, has maintained her family in the absence of her husband. But the loneliness that she suffered has become a living thing, "the years were live creatures" (241). She relies on the neighbours for emergency help with the children that Nasir should have done, she suffers the ignominy of taking monetary help from her sisters and mother. "Khawla did not forget anything she had gone through, day by day, hour by hour, minute by minute, everything inside her sapping her spirit" (241). To gainsay

Nasir's argument was not difficult for Khawla. His patriarchal attitude that he could marry and yet live with another woman, could leave his wife pregnant after each visit and compensate with phone calls after midnight or with oversized clothes for his children, because he never knew their required sizes, appear dispassionate and apathetic to Khawla and she departs from the marriage.

Presiding over these lives, is the matriarch of the family, Salima, who suffered a lot when she was young. She had been claimed by her paternal uncle Shaykh Said, after the death of her father, but there was a definite disparity in treatment between Salima and her cousins. She suffered privations and her mother was unable to alleviate her situation, since she was sent to live with her brother. Salima is allowed to move to her maternal uncle's home with her mother after her thirteenth birthday and those are the halcyon days of her life. Soon after, Shaykh Said orders her return as he has negotiated her marriage with his kinsman Azzan. When she does not agree to the marriage, mercenaries hired by Shaykh Said swim through the canal or *falaj* and enter the maternal uncle's house. After a few hours, Salima earns the title 'bride of the *falaj*' and is forced into a marriage that turns out to be reasonably successful. She loses a son, but her three daughters survive and she is happy in their marriages. When her eldest granddaughter London chooses a husband whose forefathers had been slaves to her family, Salima's sense of honour is outraged. The ingrained customs and traditions of the desert do not allow her to accept on equal terms the choice made by her grand daughter London. Slave trade is ubiquitous in the history of Oman. Zarifa is a slave, who has been working in the household of Sulyman, the merchant. Being a slave, she was married off to another slave and expected to bow down to the whims and fancies of the master who owned her. Her husband, however, had different ideas and ran off to freedom when he got the opportunity, abandoning his wife and unborn child. She has also been the resident concubine and foster mother to Abdallah. Her ancestors were brought clandestinely from Africa and sold as slaves to rich merchants. Her mother Ankabuta "grew up, after her brothers had all been sold away, as an orphan in the home of Shaykh Said" (192). The patriarchal power over the body and soul of the slave has two sides, both of which are seen in Zarifa's and her husband Habib's. While Zarifa takes over the responsibility of bringing up the infant born to Sulayman, Habib looks for his chance to flee and return to his native country from where he was forcibly taken. Even on his deathbed, Sulyman orders his son to bring back the errant slave, tie him up and thrash him for disobedience. The son, Abdallah, patiently explains that there are no slaves and that they are all free and equal in the country. This is how the author higlights that slave trade was part of the history of the country and an important factor in its economy. Zarifa manages to impose an equality in status between herself and the other women in Mayya's house when she visits them, even though she is a slave. Abdallah has known no motherly love except that of Zarifa's, yet, he is unaware that she has passed away, when he was busy with his business in Muscat. His heartfelt "I didn't know!" reveals the depth of the attachment that existed between the master and the late slave.

The rituals of routine life presented in the novel, epitomise the simple life intertwined with traditional beliefs that sometimes border on superstition. Zarifa offers food and drink to the spirits that are believed to be lurking around and waiting for a chance to do ill to the humans. When children are born, Zarifa carries a full platter and offers it to the 'Jinns' to propitiate them and request them to stay away from the new born baby and the new mother. She is constantly taking the name of the Almighty, as a prefix and suffix, to her sentences, to justify her thoughts, words and actions.

A Bedouin beauty whose name is Najiya, labelled Qamar (the moon), is enamoured of Azzan, the father of Mayya,

Asma and Khawla. He does not play any active part in the household and leaves the practicalities to his wife, Salima. The first time Qamar accosts Azzan with: "I am Najiya. I am Qamar, the Moon. It is you I want" (41) Azzan is scared and runs to the safety of his home. Relentless and beautiful Qamar, has her wish and ensnares Azzan. Their relationship fulfils the loneliness that Qamar has felt, despite her success in business and restoration of the health of her ailing brother. She is a strong character who pursues with single mindedness what she wants and obtains it. She is not cowed down by tradition nor the patriarchal society as she consolidates her position after her father's demise. Being a successful business woman in such a society incites the jealousy of others and the author does not delineate what happens to this woman in the novel, although there is a hint that Mayya suspects that her mother Salima has something to do with the disappearance of the alluring Bedouin. The novelist gives over a separate chapter "The Man in the Desert" who 'communicates with Saturn' and performs a ritual which would result in "knotting Azzan's carnal desire for Najiya" at the behest of the Bride of the *falaj* i.e. Salima. The granddaughter of Salima, London, is a modern woman, who has received good education and is a practising physician. She is pursued by her classmate and an aspiring poet, Ahmad and when she reciprocates his love, her mother and her grandmother oppose. The fidelity of young love triumphs and a marriage contract is signed and betrothal vows are exchanged between London and Ahmad. Ahmad claims that their "marriage is a victory over the disgusting hidebound class structure of society, and a crowning of true love" (232). This is another reality that the author brings to the fore, the clash of history and modernity in the form the descendant of a former slave winning the hand of the descendant of the family of owners of the slave. However, this idealised situation implodes when Ahmad becomes violent and physically abuses London. Again, the author foregrounds the reality behind the veneer of civilisation. It becomes very difficult for London to forget her near marriage and move on with life, as recommended by her friend Hannan. Hannan is yet another representative of the modern young woman who has to find a career and succeed in order to receive recognition. She is more worldly wise and brutally advises London that love is a mirage and what Ahmad had apparently given her was not the real version. Hannan had been a victim of sexual assault and London had nursed her through when she was training to be a doctor. Much as London would like to heed Hannan's words, she finds it a monumental task to 'hit the delete button on Ahmad' as suggested by Hannan.

Alharthi in this novel *Celestial Bodies,* makes the foreign familiar by providing a unique, sometimes poetic description. Combining history, descriptions of rituals and traditions, and stories that are intertwined, Alharthi presents an alluring picture of Omani society. Celestial Bodies are those that exist in a sphere beyond the reach of humans. Of all the celestial bodies, the closest celestial body to the Moon is the Earth. The phase of the Moon affects the tides on the Earth and demonstrates the movement between the high and low phases of life on this planet.

> Know that the stars of the firmament empty their gems into the moon, and the moon spills them into the water. ... The moon is a treasure house for what is on high and what lies below. The moon moves between high and low, between the sublime and the filth of creation. Of all the celestial bodies, the moon is closest to the matters of this lower world. And so it is a guide to all things. (CB 217)

When Asma is a new bride, she returns to visit her parents and sees that her father is indisposed and wants her to read a book that he pulls out from under his pillow. The passage extolls the moon:

Contemplate the state of the moon until you know it well. Its soundness is the strength of all things, its ruin the corruption of all things. If the moon moves closer to another celestial body then it gives more force to whatever that body can tell us or give us. When the moon moves away from another body in the firmament it weakens that sphere's power. (CB 217)

In his weakened state, Azzan is still pining for the exquisite Qamar. When their relationship prospered, he was in his best state. When he has separated from the moon (Qamar), partly by his choice and partly by his wife's emissary to the celestial bodies, he is at his lowest state.

When the moon's light intensifies in its approach to Mercury, that is the best state of all. But if the Moonlight is weak as it confronts Saturn, or moves closer to it, this is the worst of all worlds. (CB 217)

The power of a woman is equated to that of a celestial body and the fate of man kind hinges on their relationship with women.

Alharthi portrays the multiplicity of roles that women play and perform in the novel that is a microcosm of society: the possessive wife, the spurned lover, the unrequited lover, mother, sister, daughter, granddaughter. When the woman is free of patriarchy, she is subdued by religion and tradition, when she overcomes the obstacles of religion and tradition, her gender is held up to chain her again. Alharthi portrays how the "gender dynamics in Oman are affected by the neopatriarchal state, which are often pronatalist, emphasize sex differences and complementary roles rather than legal equality and serve to perpetuate stratification based on gender" (Haddad 144).

Crenshaw says that she has used intersectionality as a prism to examine a host of issues, conditions, policies and rhetorics even while "black feminism figured as the widely acknowledged generative source of intersectionality" (Lutz 224). She points out that it is not just about black women, as scholars have "deploy[ed] intersectionality to analyse a plethora of issues" (224) all around the globe. It is a dynamic interface of systems of power across a variety of institutions and contexts. That is the reason this tool is apt for an analysis of *Celestial Bodies* one of the first novels to be acclaimed from Oman and distinguished with the Man Booker International award. The paper catches glimpses of the various women characters that the novelist has portrayed. Each is fighting a battle of her own and winning or adapting to strike her own path, to create her own celestial orbit to revolve in. The novel undermines recurrent stereotypes, presents the changing socio-economic structures and shows how it impacts the family. Alharthi argues that the position of women is manifold and it is always a struggle to find a foothold and carve out a niche for themselves, fighting against the combined powers of gender, religion and patriarchy that is cemented by tradition.

Bibliography

Abudi, Dalya. *Mothers and Daughters in Arab Women's Literature.The Family Frontier.* Boston: Brill, 2011. Ebook.

Alharti, Jokha. *Celestial Bodies.* Trans. Marilyn Booth. New Delhi: Simon & Schuster, 2019.Print.

Ashour, Radwa, Ferial J.Ghazoul & Hasna Reda-Mekdashi. *Arab Women Writers: A Critical Reference Guide, 1873-1999.* Trans. Mandy McClure. American U Cairo P, 2008. Ebook.

Cooper, Brittney. "Intersectionality" *The Oxford Handbook of Feminist Theory* Eds. Lisa Disch & Mary Hawkesworth. Oxford: Oxford U P, 2016. Ebook.

Fayad, Mona. "Reinscribing Identity: Nation and Community in Arab Women's Writing" *College Literature,* Vol. 22, No. 1, Third World Women's Inscriptions (Feb. 1995) pp 147-160. *jstor.org.*

Haddad, Yvonne Yazbeck & John L Esposito. *Islam, Gender, & Social Change.* Oxford U P, 1998. Ebook.

Hassan, Riffat. "Feminism in Islam" *Feminism and World Religions.* Eds. Arvind Sharma & Katherine K. Young. State New York U P, 1999. Ebook.

Lutz, Helma, Maria Teresa Herrera Vivar, Linda Supik. *Framing Intersectionality: Debates on a Multi-Faceted Concept in Gender Studies.* London: Routledge, 2016. Ebook.

Rev. Issa J. Boullata. *Intersections: Gender, Nation, and Community in Arab Women's Novels* Lisa Suhair Majaj, Paula W Sunderman & Therese Saliba Eds. NY: Syracuse U P, 2002.*Digest of Middle East Studies.* Fall 2003. Web. 21 Jun. 2019.

Paludi, Michele A, J. Harold Ellens. eds. *Feminism and Religion: How Faiths View Women and Their Rights* Eds.. Santa Barbara: Praeger, 2016. Ebook.

Yuval-Davis, Nira. Intersectionality and Feminist Politics. *European Journal of Women's Studies*, SAGE Publications (UK and US), 2006, 13 (3), pp.193-209. ff10.1177/1350506806065752ff. ffhal- 00571274f. Pdf. 21 Jun. 2019.

Zeidan, Joseph T. *Arab Women Novelists: The Formative Years and Beyond.* State U NewYork P, 1995. Ebook.

Addressing Ecofeminism: A Study of *Temsula Ao and Easterine Iralu*

- Dr. Debarati Das

Bio: **Dr. Debarati Das**, Assistant Professor, Dept. of English, Handique Girls' College, Guwahati-1.

Abstract: Ecological feminism can be considered as a branch of feminism which probes into the inter-relations between women and nature. The North-Eastern states of India has a well-defined ethnic, linguistic, cultural and geographic identity. This paper aims to analyse the writings of Temsula Ao and Easterine Iralu of the north-eastern region.

Keywords: Ecofeminism, Women, Nature.

Women Writing started in the North-East with the coming of the British and also with the intrusion of the Missionaries which moved into the social and cultural system of North-East India. This resulted in the fall of north-eastern literature as a whole and to women's literature in specific. But it is also appropriate to note that during this period the contribution of women to literature revolved around children's stories and also to god-fearing or super-natural narratives. Northeast literature can be termed as 'conflict literature' because it is engulfed with mythologies and magical elements. These writers beautifully portray the concept of rootedness and rootlessness which prevails within the people of Northeast India. The position of the female community is not culturally, socially, and spiritually empowered as it has to undergo patriarchal domination. The reason for this patriarchal domination can be traced back in the age-old customs and practices of the society, which also denied economic and mental independence to women. As women are ringed in the four walled structure their contribution towards literature is very meagre.

The theory of Eco-feminism came into prominence in the twentieth century where multitudinous forms of feminist, environmental theories, and activisms were intersected. It grew as a consequence of the feminist movement of the 1960's which attempts at the intertextuality between gender and ecology from the cognitive content. In 1974, the term "ecofeminism" was conceived by Francoise d'Eaubonne as a connection of the ecology and women (Morgan,4). "Ecofeminism as a movement resists the domination of nature by humanity and also the domination of women by men, exploring the connection between the two processes and seeking a new relationship between man, woman, and nature". Plumwood brings forth the history of western philosophy in terms of dichotomy, signifying how the 'female' nature has been analytically besmirched, subjugated and demoralized. The rational zenith, which now seems impending, will be the destruction of the planet by 'the master subject' in the name of 'rational economy' and global profit, unless raison d'être can be remade. The foremost step is to develop 'the rationality of the mutual self' which would make certain 'the incomparable riches of diversity in the world's cultural and biological life' and persuade chipping in the 'community of life'

Man has attained success in all spheres of life but in this attainment of success he has completely forgotten about the ecological balance of nature which is of utmost necessity for all living organisms to survive. From time immemorial it is believed that nature is the key to our esthetical, rational, and reflective cognitive system which takes us into the world of spiritual and mental satisfaction. Nature in the contemporary scenario is taken for granted and man has intentionally exploited all the natural reserves which has resulted in destructive furies such as fani, tsunami, floods, earthquakes, landslides and other natural calamities. In general Ecofeminism portrays the deplorable condition and victimization of mother nature and women by the patriarchal society which is termed theoretically as androcentrism. Ecological feminism can be considered as a branch of feminism which probes into the inter-relations between women and nature. Its name was coined by French feminist Françoise d'Eaubonne in 1974. Ecofeminism uses the basic feminist tenet of equality between genders, a revaluing of non-patriarchal or nonlinear structures, and a view of the world that respects organic processes, holistic connections, and the merits of intuition and collaboration.

The central dichotomy constitutes of culture and nature and also of male vindication and female nature. They are raveled approaches of oppression of the human world. The way women have been devalued and denied cultural participation because of their gender, the downgrading of nature has also been disseminated through the depiction of Nature as 'female'

Nature has been represented as a woman in two rather differing senses: 'she' is identified with the body of laws, principles and processes that is the object of scientific scrutiny and experimentation. But 'she' is also nature conceived as spatial territory, as the land or earth which is tamed and tilled in agriculture (and with this we may associate a tendency to feminize viewed simply as landscape

– trees, woodlands, hills, rivers, streams, etc. are frequently personified as female or figure in similes comparing them to parts of the female body). In both these conceptions, nature is allegorized as either a powerful maternal force, the womb of all human production, or as the site of sexual enticement and ultimate seduction. Nature is both the generative source, but also the potential spouse of science, to be wooed, won, and if necessary forced to submit to intercourse. The Aristotelian philosophy, claimed Bacon, in arguing for an experimental science based on sensory observation, has 'left Nature herself untouched and invilolate'; those working under its influence had done no more than 'catch and grasp' at her, when the point was 'to seize and detain her'; and the image of nature as the object of the eventually 'fully carnal' knowing of science is frequently encountered in Enlightenment thinking and famously pictured in Louis Ernest Barrias's statue of *La Nature devoilant devant la science,* a copy of which stood in the Paris Medical faculty in the nineteenth century.(141)

The North-Eastern states of India have a well-defined ethnic, linguistic, cultural and geographic identity. This paper aims to analyse the writings of Temsula Ao and Easterine Iralu of the northeastern region.Temsula Ao is recognized as a poet whose best known collections of poetry are *Songs that Tell, Songs that Try to Say*, *Songs of Many Moods*, *Songs from Here and There,* and *Songs from the Other Life.* Temsula Ao and Easterine Iralu are both Naga poets. Temsula Ao taught English Literature at North-Eastern Hill University. She was born in Jorhat district, Assam, in 1945. She has published four books of poetry and a collection of short stories. She was also a Fulbright Fellow at the University of Minnesota during 1985-86 and was awarded the Padma Shree in 2007. Easterine Iralu on the other hand teaches literature in the University of Tromso, Norway. She was born in Kohima, Nagaland, in 1959 and has published one book of poems, a literary collection and works on the history and folk poetry of Nagaland. She was awarded the Silver Medal for Best Creative Writing in the All India Essay Contest organized by the Bertrand Russell Study Forum, 1980. Her writings are based in the realistic life of the people in Nagaland of North-East India. Apart from writing, she also performs Jazz poetry with her band Jazzpoesi. Easterine Kire published her first book of poetry *Kelhoukevira* in 1982. This is also considered as the first book of Naga poetry to be ever published in English. *A Naga Village Remembered* published in 2003 is the first novel by a Naga writer to be written in English. Her other novels are *A Terrible Matriarchy, Mari,* and *Bitter Wormwood. Don't Run, My Love* is last written in 2017. Apart from these she has also written children's books, articles and essays. Kire has also translated around 200 oral poems from her language.

In the poem *Genesis Easterine Kire* speaks of a time when she was worried about her own land and her heart was aching at the sight of confusion that was prevailing in Nagaland. She profoundly goes back to her past and cannot accept the present situation of her state and this is clearly found in the first stanza of her poem thus:

Keviselie speaks of a time
when her hills were untamed
her soil young and virgin
and her warriors worthy
the earth had felt good
and full and rich and kind to his touch. (*Genesis*, 139).

She deeply remembers about the past history of North-East India when the seven sisters were considered as one North-Eastern state which has now been divided into seven due to the political conflict and also due to the primary conflict of insurgency. This has also affected the naturalness of the Mother Earth and Kire now feels a deep sense of regret for losing the natural abundance of her state due to modernization and advancement of technologies and also due to mutilation done to Mother Earth by the so called savages. This is clearly portrayed in the second stanza of her poem:

Her daughters were seven
with the mountain air in their breath
and hair the colour of soft summer nights
Every evening they would return
their baskets overflowing
with the yield of the land
then they would gather round
and their songs filled all the earth (*Genesis* 139*)*.

Kire again shows a deep sense of longing for those lost days of the North-Eastern states when these states were filled with hills and valleys and they were undisturbed by the scientific advancement of modern society. She really yearns for the reparation of the former days of Mother Earth when it was filled with total peace and serenity. She very aptly writes this in the poem:

when she will be made whole
restored to herself again
but until such a time
yea, until winter comes
stay, stay the songs of Kelhoukevira (*Genesis* 140).

She explicitly defines that "For the story of Nagaland is the story of the Naga soul on a long, lonely jouney of pain, loss and bereavement, a silent holocaust in which words seldom were enough to carry the burden of being born a Naga. Therefore, I shall use poems to try to tell the Naga story". (Iralu. *The Conflict in Nagaland: Through a Poet's Eyes).* Iralu is of the notion that poetry is language of the soul because it reflects a person's real human feelings and emotions and also motherly feeling of the women towards the Mother Earth. She is very scared of Nagaland's natural beauty being destroyed by the technologiacl inventions that invaded the state and this she clearly describes in her poem *For Justin-Pierre*. She very clearly refers to her poetry as: "The poetry of the hills and dark, dense woods, the spirit stories that nestle in every village, the high romance of star-crossed lovers as well as of the people who turn into stars, and now, in recent years, the long holocaust of genocide, rape and torture of a gentle people"(*Should Writers Stay in Prison, 2004*). Due to the preponderant social, cultural, economic, and political condition in Nagaland Iralu is perceptive about the fate of nature in her own native state. This is very clearly portrayed in the poem *For Justin-Pierre* thus:

One day, my son,
when you come to ask me
what colour was the sky
before it turned grey
I will no longer have the answers. (*Dancing Earth*, 142).

The first story in the book *Laburnum For My Head* which is also the title of the book portrays an elderly woman's strange longing for the laburnum flowers which she obstinately wants to be planted during her lifetime. Temsula Ao beautifully thinks: "The laburnum tree on the other hand is alive and ever unchanging in its seasonal cycles: it is resplendent in May; by summer-end the stalks holding its yellow blossoms turn into brown pods; by winter it begins to look scraggly and shorn".(2) The story *Laburnum For My Head* opens very aesthetically when Ao describes the month of May which is commonly associated as a month of spring. She dramatically inscribes "Every May something extraordinary happens in the new cemetery of the sleepy little town standing beyond the southernmost corner of the vast expanse of the old cemetery- dotted with concrete vanities, both ornate and simple- the humble Indian laburnum bush erupts in glory, with its blossoms of yellow mellow beauty" (1). In this story, "Laburnum for My Head", Lentina the protagonist aspires to plant the laburnum trees which she believes that will keep her alive even after her death. To turn her dream into a reality she takes the help of her age-old driver Babu. She attaches a bond with him and makes him her secret sharer. Her inviolable secret was to fulfil her dream which becomes an 'epiphanic sensation' for her. This epiphanic sensation is to have a laburnum tree planted at her grave, one which would live on over her remains as an alternative to an ordinary tombstone. Lentina breaks all the conventional rules in order to fulfil her dream. She even despises her children and with the support of members of the town committee and the public in order to plant the laburnum tree on her tomb. Subsequently, when she is harassed by her age she becomes weak and fragile yet she does not lose hope of seeing the laburnum tree grow on her headstone. She waits all her life to see the sight of the voluptuous efflorescence on her laburnum plant. On reaching home, Lentina was very satiated with the help that Babu had done for her and blessed him for his help gesticulating an end to their relationship as if Lentina has predicted her death. After this very incident, Lentina estranged herself from her family stayed in a desolate room and retired from life very soon. After Lentina's death Ao writes thus: "And every May, this extraordinary wish is fulfilled when the laburnum tree, planted on her grave site in the new cemetery of the sleepy little town, bursts forth in all its glory of buttery-yellow splendour". (20)

The poem *Lament for an Earth* refers to the state of the Mother Earth which has diminished with the passage of time. She wistfully inscribes:

There was a forest,

Verdant, virgin, vibrant
With tall trees
In majestic splendour
Their canopy
Unpenetrated
Even by the mighty sun,
The stillness humming
With birds" cries (1-10).

The slaughter of the magnificence of the forest is equal to the withering of a woman. Here the poet depicts the relationship between Nature and woman. She portrays the grandiose of Mother Nature and depicts its severe challenges and sacrifices in the lines below:

Cry for the river
Muddy, mis-shapen
Grotesque
Chocking with the remains
Of her sister
The forest.
No life stirs in her belly now.
The bomb
And the bleaching powder
Have left her with no tomorrow (53-62).

The river and the forest according to Ao is entangled in the relationship of sisterhood. The flowing water is now at stake with the decadence of industrial revolution. The green bank of the river is now encroached with bricks and cement. The woman and Mother Nature congruity is inscribed in *Requim*:

Who will mourn this blackened mass?
This charred carcass
Of a recent blushing bride
Roasted on the pyre ...

...And abetted
By the kitchen stove.
Who will mourn? (1-11)

The above lines in the poem describe how a new bride is tortured by her in-laws for want of material wealth. Added to this Ao also compares a newly wedded bride with all her fresh dreams to a land that hopes for a bright tomorrow. The bride can be considered as a metaphor for the nature of Northeast, and the patriarchal society can be viewed as the members of the industrial world, whose gluttony has engulfed the serenity of our Mother Nature. Added to this, Donna Haraway a critic of biology and a supporter of nature promisingly writes:

In the belly of the local/global monster in which I am gestating, often called the postmodern world, global technology appears to *denature* everything, to make everything a malleable matter of strategic decisions and mobile production and reproduction processes. Technological decontextualization is ordinary experience for hundreds of millions if not billions of human beings, as well as other organisms. I suggest that this is not a denaturing so much as a *particular production* of nature. (*Promises* 297)

The utter worries for the fate of Ao's Mother Nature shows her motherly love which is portrayed in *To the Children of the World*. Women are perceived to bring in new life to this world. Therefore, as mothers they are concerned to provide a green ambiance to their new born. But with so much of desecration Ao doubts the greenness of the Mother Earth:

To all you children who are born,
And are yet to be born, ...
Why you were born
To inherit

The plunder of the ages... (1-8)

Temsula Ao's nature poems raise a strong resistance to the paraphernalia of change that are responsible for the destruction of Mother Nature. In the poem, *Earthquake*, she gives a warning to the society as well as patriarchy which denatures both Mother earth and woman:

When the earth rumbles
And controts
To throw up her secret
Like a pregnant woman
After conception,
It is no portent
Of new life.
But of death and disaster
For those who dwell
Upon her swell (1-10).

Deleuze and Guattari in the realm of politics writes:

But once again so much caution is needed to prevent the plane of consistency from becoming a pure plane of abolition or death, to prevent the involution from turning into a regression to the undifferentiated. Is it not necessary to retain a minimum of strata, a minimum of forms and functions, a minimal subject from which to extract materials, affects, and assemblages?... It is, of course, indispensable for women to conduct a molar politics, with a view to winning back their own organism, their own history, their own subjectivity: 'we as women...' makes its appearance as a subject of enunciation. But it is dangerous to confine oneself to such a subject, which does not function without drying up a spring or stopping a flow....It is thus necessary to conceive of a molecular women's politics that slips into molar confrontations, and passes under or through them. (276-278)

Earthquake is perceived as the vindication taken on human civilization by the Mother Earth. Ao portrays the image of Mother Earth as a pregnant woman who conceives to devastate life by bringing out the basalt from its abyss.

She gaps open
To devour
Toppled towers
And torn limbs...
Mountains to slide,
Rivers to rise
And volcanoes
To vomit
Lava and deadly ash.
She heaves and hurtles
As if to uproot
The very moorings
Of life (11-20).

Here, we can remember, Wordsworth's poetry where men have gone astray from Mother Nature because of their humdrum desires against nature. Hartman himself states that Wordsworth perceives Mother Nature as "a presence and a power," not an object, and that the poet's "sense of mission" is to protect the earth because the human imagination needs to coexist physically and intellectually with it (*Romance* 290).

Indu Swami states that:

This image of the Mother Earth as the destroyer also matches the image of *Ma Durga* found in the Hindu Mythology. *Ma Durga* possesses different images in different situations. She is usually known for her *Shanti Roop* (peace image), *Matri Roop* (mother image) and *Daya Roop* (mercy image). But when the *Mahisasura* dared to destroy her creation and hurled violence on her people, the peaceful, merciful, mother took the violent forms of *Chandi, Rudra* and *Shakti* (all three images represents violent and fearful image of *Devi Durga*) and beheaded the monster to bring peace to the earth. This analogy comes to the reader's mind since *Prakiti* (Nature) is an image of *Devi Durga*. The ending of the poem again blends the image of a woman and with that of nature:

And after her fearsome furore
Is registered
On the Richter scale
She subsides
Like a hysterical female
After her fury is spent
Leaving...
That he has
 Only this unpredictable
 And temperamental Earth
To love And content with (25-39).

Mother Nature is poetically compared with woman and Ao gives an admonition to the human world to preserve the destroying Nature. Temsula Ao through her poems shows the necessity to safeguard and nurture Mother Nature for our posterity. In a similar vein, in the poem *The Garden,* Ao inscribes:

A slice of the earth
On the ground,
 Or firmed in pots
Of any imaginable Size, shape and colour
Becomes the respectable
 For new life (1-7).
[...]
They grow Goaded by hormone,
Aided by fertilizers And tended by your loving care (14-17).

The quaint Mother Earth figure takes the interpreter into the hackneyed society where the mother nurtures the child with her own way of nourishment. Wordsworth expands "maternal love to natural adoption and ideas of interconnectedness in the biosphere. He goes on admiring the greatness of maternal and natural love: From this beloved presence—there exists A virtue which irradiates and exalts All objects through all intercourse of sense. No outcast he, bewildered and depressed; Along his infant veins are inter fused The gravitation and the filial bound Of nature that connect him with the world". (258-264)

Mother Nature and literature from ancient times have an intimate relationship which is portrayed in all the various works of art. Literature is an embodiment of natural scenario which pageants human fervour for the environment and also portrays but also illustrate human deportment towards Mother Nature. But with the passage of time Mother Nature and human mother though idolized is oppressed and abused to the core. The state of human existence and liaison which is interconnected with Mother Nature of Nagaland and entwined with supernatural power is portrayed beautifully by Temsula Ao though it is not related to the contemporary civilization:

Stone people
 The worshipper
Of unknown, unseen
Spirits
Of trees and forests
 Of stones and rivers,
Believers of soul
And its varied forms,
Its sojourn heir
 And passage across the water
Into the hereafter (42-52).

Temsula Ao also delineates the need of companionship which is expected by humans, non-humans and nature alike. In the poem *Songbird* one can find the need of camaraderie which is expected by both the genders also. She longs for her soulmate and loneliness engulfs her when she cannot find one of the same. A mounting disappointment surrounds her while She runs everywhere in search of a companion to share her innermost feelings but finds desolation everywhere.

The little songbird wakes up
to an eerie void, and is instantly alarmed;
no songbirds' melodies greet the morning,
only a great silence pervades the looming.

She looks for her song mates
but discovers only a vast aloneness
and wonders with mounting fear
what caused all the others to disappear.

She flits from branch to branch
in the abandoned woods
looking for a perch to sing
and call her songfriends back.

Sitting weary on a branch top
she tries to sing some old tunes
but the growing fear chokes her
and the songbird can sing no more.

She is frantic now, hopping
from one desolate branch to another
still trying to sing an old refrain
that every other songbird would know.

But no songs chant on her lips
as they lie dying within
her stricken heart that grieves
for the lost melodies.

She loses all her hope and tries to remember and enchant
about her nostalgic times but no one is able to hear reply to
her and she lies grief-stricken in her nest. She leaves her own
destination and travels far and wide so that her age-old
traditions and customs can survive till perpetuity. But she
fails in her ambition and is filled with the patriarchal
surroundings where she feels forsaken and abandoned.

She leaves the songless desert
and flies off far and wide in search
of old comrades so that
the old songs can live again.

Low in spirit and weak in body
she prolongs her weary search
until she stumbles on a curious space:
the habitat of the two-legged aliens.

In the surreal surroundings,
she spies her former mates
strutting on glittering bars inside gilded cages
trying to sing their old songs!

But there is no soul in the new songs
no harmony trilled in the voices,
no joy glinted in the eyes
and no rhythm frolicked on the feathers.

What they sing now are pathetic travesties
of the soul-filled melodies
they used to sing as unfettered songbirds.
and she knows her songbird-life is over.

Her old world has vanished;
free songs forsaken, song places abandoned,
and former songmates turned to total strangers
strutting and screeching in bonded splendours.

So into the mist of the great unknown
the broken-hearted songbird embarks on
a final journey, content to be a tiny temporary speck
in the limitless freeways of the firmament,
far away from all things that glittered.

Ecological feminism in general means the deprivation of females and exploitation of Mother Nature by the capitalist society, a concept which is based on the attitudes of patriarchy. Though she cannot go back to her world of fantasy, she tries to adjust with the conventional patriarchal world and remains content with her present world.

If women have been associated with nature, and each denigrated with reference to the other, it may seem worthwhile to attack the hierarchy by reversing the terms, exalting nature, irrationality, emotion and the human or non-human body as against culture, reason and the mind. Some ecofeminists, especially those promoting 'radical ecofeminism' and goddess worship, have adopted this approach. Thus, for example, Sharon Doubiago asserts that 'ecology consciousness is traditional woman consciousness'; 'Women have always thought like mountains, to allude to Aldo Leopold's paradigm for ecological thinking ...Charlene Spretnak similarly grounds a kind of women's spirituality in female biology and acculturation that is comprised of the truths of naturalism and the holistic proclivities of women'(26-27)

Eco-feminism blames the androcentric doubleness between man and woman. It differentiates men from women on the basis of some supposed eminence for example larger brain size, and this characteristic makes men superior over women. Ecofeminism as a concept carves up a common 'logic of domination'(Warren) and that ' women have been associated with nature, the material, emotional, and the particular, while men have been associated with culture, the nonmaterial, the rational, and the abstract'(Davion). Added to this, this concept suggests a universal cause between feminists and ecologists. Eco-feminists who have an idealistic bearing beautifully summits that 'a truly feminist perspective cannot embrace either the feminine or the masculine uncritically, but requires a critique of gender roles, and this critique must include masculinity and femininity' (Davion 9).

Works Cited

1. Ao, Temsula. "A Strange Place." Songs That Tell. Kolkata: Writers Workshop, 1988. Print.
2. "Blessings." Songs That Tell. Kolkata: Writers Workshop, 1988. Print.
3. "Death." Songs That Try to Say. Kolkata: Writers Workshop, 1992. Print.
4. "Dying." Songs That Try to Say. Kolkata: Writers Workshop, 1992. Print.
5. "Earthquake." Songs That Try to Say. Kolkata: Writers Workshop, 1992. Print.
6. "Identity and Globalization: A Naga Perspective." *Indian Folklife* 22, 2006. Web. 22 May

2014. "Lament for an Earth." Songs That Tell. Kolkata: Writers Workshop, 1988. Print.

7. "Laburnum For My Head". New Delhi: Penguin Books, 2009. Print.

8. "Requiem?" Songs That Tell. Kolkata: Writers Workshop, 1988. Print.

9. "Stone People from Lungterok." Songs That Try to Say. Kolkata: Writers Workshop, 1992. Print.

10. "The Garden." Songs That Try to Say. Kolkata: Writers Workshop, 1992. Print.

11. "To the Children of the World." Songs That Try to Say. Kolkata: Writers Workshop,   1992. Print.

12. Coupe, Laurence(ed). *The Green Studies Reader: From Romanticism to Ecocriticism,*

Canada: Routledge,2000. Print.

13. Davion, V. "Is Ecofeminism feminist?" *Ecological Feminism.* Ed. K.Warren. London:

Routledge, 1994. Print.

14. Deleuze, Gilles, and Felix Guattari. *Capitalism and Schizophrenia* (trans. Brian Massumi), Minneapolis, MN: Minnesota University Press, 1987. Print.

15. Garrard, Greg. *Ecocriticism.* Canada: Routledge, 2012. Print.

16. Haraway, Donna. *Simians, Cyborgs, and Women:The Reinvention of Nature,* New York:Routledge, 1992. Print.

17. Hartman, Geoffrey. "The Romance of Nature and the Negative Way." Romanticism and

Consciousness. Ed. Harold Bloom. New York: Norton, 1970.

18. Iralu, Easterine Kire. "The Conflict in Nagaland Through A Poet's Eyes". 2004

19. <http://nagas.sytes.net/-kaka/articles/art007.html>.ac.on 04.08.2011.

20. "Should Writers Stay in Prisons of Invisible Prisons". 2004.

21. <http://nagas.sytes.net/-kaka/articles/art007.html>.ac.on 04.08.2011.

22. Morgan, J. *Ecofeminism an emerging social movement.* Unpublished Plan B paper, Anthropology Department, University of Minnesota, Minneapolis, MN,1992. Print.

23. Plumwood, Val. *Feminism and the Mastery of Nature.* London: Routledge, 1993. Print.

24. Soper, Kate. "Naturalized Woman and Feminised Nature." *The Green Studies Reader: From Romanticism to Ecocriticism.* Ed. Laurence Coupe. Canada: Routledge, 2000. Print

25. Swami, Indu. "Tarnishing the Purity of Nature = Defloration of Woman: Analyzing Interconnections between Nature and Women in Temsula Ao's Poetry" *International Journal on Studies in English Language and Literature (IJSELL).* Volume 2 Issue 8, August 2014: 135-148. Print.

26. Warren, K(ed). *Ecological Feminism.* London: Routledge,1994. Print.

Depiction of Rural Nepal in Manjushree Thapa's Novel *The Tutor of History*

- Dr. Dipika V. Kolambe

Bio: **Dipika V. Kolambe** teaches Business Communication to undergraduate students at B.K.Birla College, Kalyan. She has a Ph.D in English and has qualified SET and NET.Her area of interest is Nepali literature in English. She has a couple of research papers published on her area of research.

Abstract:
This research paper focuses on the state of affairsin the village,Khaireni Tar, Tanahun district, West Nepal of 1990s which is portrayed in the second novel of Manjushree Thapa, *The Tutor of History*(2001).The researcher tries to analyse the socio-cultural reality of Nepali rural life such as ins and outs of the elections in the village like corruption and votes being bought or voters cajoled; and various caste and class based social groups in the village such as Khadaka,Gurung, Magar, Chettri and Bahun. This paper attempts to analyse the realistic contemporary factors of native Nepal which influence and always circumscribe the human life and its activities.In the process of scrutinizing the depiction of rural Nepal in all its messy politicization, paper also shows the truth about the native people of Nepal. Khaireni Tar's geographical locale and twilight of cultures are also examined in the paper. The paper also explores how social, political and cultural backgrounds become the setting of the novel to make a moving story of ordinary people in a

changing society of village who crave for their intimacy and meaning. The study of characters in the setting of rural Nepal is also at the locus of the paper as characters are the case studies of social and cultural realities of rural Nepal in Thapa's narrative. Rishi is one of the focal characters in the novel who represents outsiders of Khaireni Tar. Binita is a case of a woman who independently runs a teashop at the middle of bazaar. Thakalni-amma is proprietor at a local restaurant bar. Giridhar represents ordinary people of Khaireni Tar who dreamfor higher life but struggle in the day to day life because of the lack of opportunities. The uniqueness of this research paper is its analysis of Manjushree Thapa's notion of contemporary native Nepal and her interest in the conflict between tradition and modernity at social and cultural level.

Keywords: Rural Society, Native, Local, Modernity, Traditional, Cultural landscape

1990s was the period when Nepal was caught amidst the political upheaval, clashes between the King's royal rule and Maoist rebel which resulted in the making of a democratic country with an electoral process and elected government. End of the Royal policy and the liberation from the Maoist revolt brought the country on to a different phase. Nepal redefined itself with a move fromMonarchy to Democracy. Susequently, the election became the pivotal factor in Nepal. This period of emerging new Nepal is portrayed in Manjushree Thapa's novel *The Tutor of the History*. Thapadescribes the real picture of contemporary rural Nepal with its political greed, bribery, the unrestrained behaviour of politicians and insincerity of people which are the socio-political realities of the nation. These aspects are primarily played out in terms of the political situation in the novel because in Nepal, as in other underdeveloped nations, politics plays an important role in the life of its voters.

Election does not assure that the politicians are sincere and innocent. Like in other countries, in Nepal too higher authorities misuse their power and appoint criminals and guilty people on higher posts. This is revealed in the incident when Rishi is reading the newspaper and finds the news about the appointment of the new Chief for the government election commission and who was once a criminal:

The caretaker government had just appointed a new chief for the election commission. Rishi recognized the man's name, and thought back to himself, years ago, spending foggy winter mornings in a room full of thieves, murderers, rapists and activists, all huddled back-to-back on the cold dust floor. The new chief of the Election Commission had been in the Panchayat government when Rishi was jailed during a students' demonstration for democracy. Now, a decade later, the man was back in power, administering elections. (Thapa 11)

Rishi has shifted from Kathmandu to Khaireni Tar and thus represents the social and cultural dislocation. He is born in a village and afterwardsshifted to a city and consequently he remains as an outsider to the village and a stranger to the city because of his difficulty in rejecting the rural culture and accepting urban one. Rishi's identity is negligible in urban place and hence he searches for an identity. Although he is now in small village, he has his unique self: "His presence in the city was slim. In his birth village he had a fuller identity – he was so-and-so's grandson, so-and-so's son, a member of a select caste and class – but in Kathmandu he was anonymous, a slip of a man like all the others, a shadow moving against a wall and disappearing when the sky clouded over (Thapa12-13)."

Giridhar and Thakali-aama represent the culture of alcohol consumption in Khaireni Tar. Giridhar goes to Thakalni-aama's restaurant to fetch a bottle of White Horse. Instead, she serves KhukuriRum, a local drink to him. Thapa describes the scene of alcohol consumption vividly: "He took out a quarter-bottle of Khukuri Rum from his shirt pocket, took a long swig from it, and tucked it away. Then he turned back to the rain. So much rain. If all the rain shimmering down beyond his front porch –if all this rain were vodka! The whole world would be afloat" (Thapa 15). Thapa also describes rural Nepali houses and how Nepali women decorate their homes with artistic things made by them. These objects turn into the cultural markers of the community in the rural Nepal which suggest the women-centred hobby such as embroidery and house decoration: "With great vigour, Asha wiped the mirror's gilt frames, the cotton-covered sofa, the coffee table and its cut-glass ashtray, the television set covered with a needlepoint scarf, and the embroidery on the wall that read, in English, WELL-COME HOME SWEET HOME" (Thapa34).

Sani, the young orphan girl who lives with Binita, is a testimony tothe dangers of living in village with its lack of health programs and struggle with so many diseases: *"Having survived the usual dangers of mumps, measles, rubella,* diphtheria, meningitis, whooping cough, polio, tetanus, typhoid and hepatitis A, and the after-effects of malnutrition and neglect (for she was orphaned young)," (Thapa 38).

Caste consciousness is another social aspect of the rural Nepali society. Khaireni Tar's Caste system gets into the core of electoral process: "There was talk among those gathered beneath the bar-peepal tree that the ethnic-rights Janamukti party might also field a candidate: a Gurung-

Magar man would voice the resentment of the minorities towards Chettri-Bahun caste domination" (Thapa 42).

In man-woman relationship, which is a key social institution in Thapa's narrative, rejection of love by the girl has many meanings and cultural shades in the Khaireni Tar. In patriarchal society man is always the superior to woman. Sani rejects HarshaBahadur, a Khadaka boy which upsets Harsha who is conditioned by patriarcal mindset:

Rejection was the swift dive you took when slipping on bamboo leaves: no time to reach out for balance. Rejection was the stench of rotten feed that cows had urinated on. Rejection sounded like an old witch laughing at a naked boy. How swiftly it moved, rejection, a sudden hailstorm pelting down from calm blue skies.
 (Thapa 96-97)

People in Khaireni Tar believe in religion and mantra to the point of being superstitious. Even political leaders start their campaign with mantra to create a compromise between tradition and rationalism. Thapa, with a touch of satire depicts the ritual:
Thankfully, the gayatri mantra gave a man a chance to purify himself. Om bhoorbhubasubaha, the ascetic chanted all day, willing his atma towards all-pervasive Brahma. Om tatsabiturbarenyam. Only the gayatri mantra could cleanse a man of base hungers. For wrongdoing began in the stomach; the stomach was the cause of all evil. Bhargodebasyadhimahi, the ascetic chanted. Dhiyoyonaprachodayat. He lifted his shirt to watch his stomach move, like ocean waves undulating. Only when every politician mastered his stomach would the country be liberated from corruption. Om (Thapa110-111).

Despite subscribing to the ideology of progressive or revolutionary parties, people in Kaireni Tar do not leave their religious beliefs. Most of them think that lord Krishna will redeem them from troubles. Jimmawal-baaje explains how religion is integral in election politics. He gives an interpretation of people which explains their blind devotion: "People have gods in them. These gods – the deities in us – they deserve more attention that stone idols, don't you feel?" (Thapa 142)

Though Khaireni Tar is a multi-ethnic and multicultural location, one community feels its ethnic culture is superior to the others. Though Khaireni Tar represents multilingual culture, languages also have their hierarchic status. Local parties are divided along the lines of linguistic differences. Ethnic differences create conflict in Khaireni Tar:"In every political party, in every organization, in every government office, in all sectors of society, Chettri-Bahun castes hold power while the ethnic Sherpa, Tamang, Magar, Gurung, Rai, Limbu people remain suppressed in the hills, and other ethnic groups remain oppressed in the southern tarai plains" (Thapa220).

Villages have their unique importance in Nepal's politics. Manjushree Thapadepicts the reality of election in Nepal as a thematic device to explore this rural scenario:"Most of the electorate lay south of the river. The most remote villages were three days' walk away; but the group would stop at each village and take weeks wending their way through the southern area" (Thapa254).

Rural economy is made weak by poverty and the lack of day to day requirements. People live hopelessly because of this kind poverty in the village: "No one looked at Kami villages, generations-old sharecroppers who were entangled in debt, their self-esteem trampled on by centuries of bigotry" (Thapa263-264).

There is the local awareness programme in village launched by the educated women as they come Khaireni Tar. They motivate women to join party and form women's groups such as mother's group and literacy group. These groups help to motivate local women to live free and happy; they dance, sing and share their happiness and sorrows. Binita, Thakalni-aama, Phool Devi, Bazaar women and the lower caste women gather, reflecting the enthusiasm of these groups: "Thirty, forty of us getting together and creating a ruckus. Come and see.' She admonished some women passing by with basketsful of dung. 'Are you so busy you can't come with us? Have you no time for fun? What, you're carrying the weight of the whole world on your backs?'" (Thapa 287).

Nepali villages are affected by natural disasters because of their geographical situation. In Khareni Tar, there is always the terror of natural disaster. Thapa reveals the situation while focalizing Rishi's character: "He kept listening to the radio, fixing on whatever news he could find. Unseasonal floods, mudslides, earthquakes measuring seven on the Richter scale: a catalogue of disasters" (*TH* 349)

Festivals are the most significant cultural element in Khaireni Tar. Tihar is the well-known festival celebrated in the Nepal. Gods, cats, crows and relatives are worshipped during this festival to show their gratitude towards nature, animals and birds: "'Tripti cried, tossing rice towards the ravens perched on the banana plants. 'Here, kaag, this is for you. Eat some rice'" (Thapa360). Thapa adds: "The four of them remained on the porch feeding birds, almost as though they were a family." (*TH* 360)

Thapa illustrates that Khaireni Tar has corruption, rigging, violence and malpractices during election. She describes how new democracies are seen through the eyes of international observers:

Three foreigners got out of the vehicles, accompanied by Nepali officials from a human rights organization. While the officials went to talk to the election officers, the foreigners stared uncertainly around them. There was an Indian woman, a British man and an American woman. The American woman produced a camera from her handbag and took picture of children who had gathered to stare at them. (Thapa 440)

Nepal's rural culture is conservative and man-woman relationship is not an exception to that. To fall in love with opposite sex before marriage is a taboo in rural Nepal. Rishi indicates that perhaps the new democracy becomes the tool to make men and women feel free to express love. His words also indicate the awakening of feminism in Nepal in the context of rural society. These words also contextualize issues such as choice, desire and love of rural Nepali women:

...it turned out I was being undemocratic in not giving you any choice but to love me. It's all my fault, I now know. I wanted love but didn't care if you wanted to give it. But a girl needs a choice. A girl needs freedom, a girl needs to make up her own mind. It turns out that that's what democracy means. (Thapa 449)

Thapa's novel ends with a revolutionary note which reflects the new face of rural Nepal. Rishi wants to marry Binita and this act is a gesture of emerging Nepal which accepts widow remarriage. *The Tutor of History* is a depiction of the changing culture rural Nepal and its socio-political dynamics. Thapa seems to implicate that Nepal's transition from monarchy to democracy controls the lives of people in the village, Khaireni Tar and that it will also empower rural women with their participation in the electoral process, economic opportunities and widow remarriage.

Work Cited

Thapa, Manjushree. *The Tutor of History*. New Delhi: Penguin Books, 2001.

Ecological Concerns and Novelistic Art of Virginia Woolf's *The Voyage Out*

— Dr. (Smt.) G. D. Ingale

Bio: Dr. G. D. Ingale is an Associate Professor and has put in 29 years of experience in Devchand College, Arjunnagar, Dist: Kolhapur, Maharashtra. She has written textbook units and self-instruction material for students which have been published by affiliated university; has nearly 20 research articles published in international journals and completed UGC funded Minor Research Project. She has been appointed as a Member, International Advisory Editorial Board in Linguistics, Cambridge Scholars Publishing, Cambridge in 2018. She is the recipient of Manini Award.

ABSTRACT:

Virginia Woolf is a novelist with 'modern' sensibility in the sense that her experimentation with the novel form includes the voice of the Nature too. *The Voyage Out* is her first novel, but it is written with an unusual sense of the organic unity between man and nature. In the days of British imperialism, she raises her voice in the novel against the same with a warning about its disastrous consequences for the existence of human life on the Earth. The novel tells the story of a young woman and her sudden death on an expedition up a tropical river in the Santa Marina Island. Woolf's ecological concerns are reflected not only in the content, but in the formal aspects of the novel too such as plot construction, characterization, setting, imagery and symbolism. Woolf's philosophy of life includes her attitude towards nature.she accords superior status to nature and portrays it as existing independent of human beings, shaping and influencing their lives. Nature is humanized and demands to be treated with respect. Her novel reveals ecofeminist concerns too.

Keywords: ecology, experimentation, imperialism, novelistic art

Academicians have studied many aspects of Virginia Woolf's (1882-1941) novels. However, her concern for nature and the relationship between man and nature remained unexplored until the end of the 20th century. Elizabeth Waller (2000; quoted in Kostokovska (2013) studies Woolf's 'process of environmental awakening' and her development of 'an entirely different form of narrative that linguistically suggests an ecology beyond the backyard- a pulsing rhythm within an ecology of language'. Charlotte Zoe Walker (2000; quoted in Kostokovska (2013) defines Woolf's relationship with nature as a conservation which she discovers at the core of Woolf's search for a language better suited to her novels. Bonnie Kime Scott traces in *Virginia Woolf and the Uses of Nature*(2007; quoted in Kostokovska (2013) Woolf's relationship to 'others in nature' from her early diaries to the garden in *To The Lighthouse* and nature in *The Waves*. She concludes that Woolf questions abuses of living beings and 'constructs solidarity across distant species'. Justyna Kostkowska in *Ecocriticism and Women Writers* (2013) presents ecological reading of her form and that of her influence on contemporary British women writers. A few others discovered in depth connections between Woolf's narrative practice and her relationship with the non-human. The present study analyses her first novel,*The Voyage Out*(1915), from the point of view of ecological concerns.

One of the aspects of her novel, among others, which makes her a distinctive novelist, is the problem of not only the survival of humanity in the era of competitive capitalism but also of the survival of the Earth in an era of intense exploitation of nature. She was living in the era when imperialism was at its peak and England was the mistress of approximately two thirds of the habitable world. She achieves this purpose in the novel by presenting nature in the following ways:

1. Nature has independent existence irrespective of its inhabitants.
2. Nature is eternal whereas human life is temporary.
3. Nature influences the course of human life.
4. The unnatural ambition of man to conquer nature/alien territories in the name of imperialism and exploiting the same for materialistic pursuits is disastrous for both Man and nature.

The Voyage Out, is set in the Edwardian era when England was the largest empire and a maritime power. It used to send ships across the globe laden with goods and men to its distantcolonies. MrVinrace, one of the characters in the novel, owns ten cargo ships plying the Atlantic Oceanwhich are all at the sea. His daughter, Rachael Vinrace, a 24 year old girl, is the heroine of the novel. It is the story of this London girl, who goes on a voyage on her father's ship to a South American island, Santa Marina,and dies suddenly at the end. It is also a love story- between Rachael and Terence Hewitt, an aspiring novelist and an Oxford don-which is cut short by her untimely death. After her death, the clouds gather- '...a gust of cold air came through the open windows, a light flashed, followed by a clap of thunder right over the hotel. The rain swished with it and the storm. In the hotel, people assembled, played chess, knitted' (*The Voyage Out*, 1992; hereafter *VO*: 351. All references to the text are from this edition). It was Rachael's *voyage out* of home, out of London and out of the world into nothingness.

This deceptively straightforward narrative is imbued with Woolf's ecological concerns in its formal aspects. The structure of the novel is unconventional. On the surface, the events appear to have been arranged in chronological order. For instance, the voyage of 'Miss Rachel Vinrace, aged twenty four' on 'her father's ship' (p.7); her aunt, Helen finding her 'incompetent' (p.13); then the fatal 'kiss' by Richard (p.66); Helen's decision to take Rachel to Santa Marina, for 'a complete course of instruction in the feminine graces' (p.77); the trip up a river as Mrs. Flushing wants to 'see the natives in their camps' (p.222); Rachel's declaration of love for Terence (266); their subsequent engagement (p.274); Rachel falling ill soon after due to headache (p.304); and her sudden death due to the heat of the tropical sun (p.334).

This apparently humanistic story of Rachael is directly influenced by cosmic forces such as the storm, the heat of the tropical sun and the island. For instance, it is the storm which causes vacillation of the ship and the fatal kiss by Richard Dalloway which makes the 24 year 'innocent' heroine feel the pangs of love culminating in her love for Terence Hewet.The tropical island, is a summer retreat for English people during winter season. It is indeed an inferno where the sun beats hot rays. Rachael dies due to the unbearable heat on the island.Woolf prepares the readers for her death by frequent references to the increasing heat that would claim its victim: 'The day increased in heat as they drove up the hill' (p.81); 'The midday sun ... was beginning to beat down hotly. ... Expeditions in such heat are perhaps a little unwise' (p.119); 'She went to the wash-stand and began sponging her cheeks with cold water; for they were burning hot' (p.233); 'The afternoon was very hot, so hot that the breaking of the waves on the shore sounded like the repeated sigh of some exhausted creature' (p.308); 'Ice-cold at first, it soon became as hot as the palm of her hand' (p.310); 'The heat was suffocating. At last the faces went farther away ...' (p.332).Rachael dies (p.341). This naturalistic explanation of death by heat arguably justifies itself as no amount of love or passion could interfere and stop it.Humanity is left to wonder about the meaning of life and death. Evelyn exclaims, 'Death, I mean. ...*What did matter then? What was the meaning of it all?* (p.346). The narrative incoherence, as pointed out by David Daiches -'no complications' (Daiches,1952: 492), Clive Bell 'discrepancy between the comic and tragic parts' (quoted in Mujumdar and Mclaurin, 1975:65) is intentional and is caused not by human agency, but by natural agency which is beyond the control of human beings.

Woolf's novelistic aesthetic is informed by the central vision of the organic unity between humans and nature. The central character, Rachel, embodies this organic unity whereas other characters, including her lover, exhibit aspects of egocentrism, materialism and worldliness. Helen, her aunt, is a 'normal' housewife who wants to lead an 'ordered' life. She wishes to 'educate' Rachael in worldly manners. Terence Hewet, the 27 year novelist, exhibits his manly ego by underestimating Rachael's musical talent and the inner cravings of her heart. In contrast, Woolf reveals the inner being of Rachael. Her spirit is one with Nature: 'Inextricably mixed in dreamy confusion, her mind seemed to enter into communion, to be delightfully expanded and combined with *the spirit of the whitish boards on deck, with the spirit of the sea, with the spirit of Beethoven*, ... (29, italics supplied); 'I feel like a fish at the bottom of the sea'(p.155); 'It seemed to her now that ... she wanted many more things than the love of one human being– *the sea, the sky* (285, italics supplied); 'She remembered their quarrels, ... and she thought how often they would quarrel in the thirty, or forty, or fifty years in which they would be living in the same house together, ... *But all this was superficial*, and had nothing to do with the life that went on beneath her eyes, ... for *that life was independent of her*, and *independent of everything else. ... She was independent of him; she was independent of everything else...She wanted nothing else.*' (p 298, italics supplied). Rachel's autonomous spirit, which she ironically discovers after she fell in love, is in contact with the primordial forces andnecessitates her union with them through death rather than her romantic union with Terence. Her life is her education in the vital powers of nature. She gradually realizes the transience of human life and eternity of time and nature: 'And life, what was that? It was only a light passing over the surface and vanishing, as in time she would vanish, though the furniture in the room would remain...She was overcome with awe that things should exist at all...' (p. 114).It was the storm and the sea that awaken her inner being to the highest point, enabling her to undergo enlargement of her soul and spiritual powers. Thus, Rachel's character becomes a symbol of unity and harmony between human and natural forces.

In the choice of themes for *The Voyage Out*, as in the later novels, Woolf is guided by the deeper significance of things which manifests itself in the form of duality between order and chaos, life and death, degradation of modern materialistic world and the inner cravings of the human heart, the eternity of nature and the human insignificance. Several utterances illustrate this: 'This reticence– this isolation– that's the matter with modern life!' (66); 'a certain dryness of the soul' (84); 'bodies without souls' (107); 'the universal silence' (114); 'chaos triumphant, things happening for no reason at all' (209); 'why was it that relations between different people were so unsatisfactory, so fragmentary so hazardous ...' (178); 'would there ever be a time when the world was one and indivisible?' (279). These reveal Woolf's agonizing cry for cosmic unity.

Nature provides the context for the narrative of the novel not only by providing geographical setting- the sea and the island for the action, but contributing to the central thematic concern of the novel viz. the existential need for the well-being of Mother Earth in the context of exploitative imperialism as nature is the cradle of human civilization. Woolf emphasizes the interdependence of human and natural world; the vastness, eternity and mystery of Nature in comparison with the smallness, insignificance and evanescence of human life; and above all, the power of nature to influence the course of events and even to strike a cruel blow indiscriminately to human life. These assertions make it amply clear: 'The wind at night blowing over the hills and woods was purer ..., more mysterious than *the earth coloured and divided by roads and fields*' (100); 'Before them they beheld an immense space– ... A river ran across the plain, ... *They felt themselves very small* ... (120)'; here the view was one of infinite sun-dried earth, earth pointed in pinnacles, heaped in vast barriers, ... earth chequered by day and night, and *partitioned into different lands, where famous cities were founded* ...' (194); 'Does it ever seem to you, Terence, that the world is composed of *vast blocks of matter and that we're nothing but patches of light*– ...? (276).

The main characters glimpse into the world of the South American jungle, the setting for the declaration of love between Terence and Rachel and realize Nature's insensitivity towards and its interference with human life. As they go up the river, the chaos of the jungle undermines their sense of the natural world as an ordered and purposive setting for their own lives. St. John Hirst voices this concern when he says, 'These trees get on one's nerves– it's all so crazy. God's undoubtedly mad. What sane person could have conceived a wilderness like this, ...' (260). All the characters are overwhelmed by this sense of human vulnerability to the hostile forces of nature. No wonder then, Rachel's death by heat, soon after their sojourn up the river, proves this thesis. Nature,thus, emerges as structural necessity in the novel.

Woolf's indictment of British imperialism is clear in the statements scattered over the novel. Woolf briefly narrates the story of the British occupation of the island: 'Three hundred years ago five Elizabethan baroques had anchored where now the *Euphrosyne* now floated. ... 'The country was still a virgin land behind a veil'. Later the English sailors bore away bars of silver, bales of linen, timbers of cedar wood, golden crucifixes knobbed with emeralds. ... The English 'greedy for flesh' 'fingers itching for gold' soon reduced the natives to a state of superstitious wonderment. A settlement was made; women were imported; children grew.... the English dwindled away...Somewhere about the middle of 17th century, the British colony came to an end except a few men, a few women and perhaps a dozen dusky children. English history then denies all knowledge of the place. ...In the last 10 years the English across the sea founded a small colony on the island.... (79-81).Woolf comments in the novel, 'One thinks of all we've done, ...and how we've gone on century after century, sending out boys from little country villages– and of men like you, Dick, and it makes one feel as if one couldn't bear not to be English! Think of *the light* burning over the House, Dick! When I stood on deck just now I seemed to see it. It's what one means by London' (42).The theme of England's colonization of the world, which, at the metaphorical level, amounts to colonization of human spirit by materialistic forces imprisoning and destroying it resulting in 'certain dryness of the soul' (84).

Woolf exposes the modern world and its materialistic civilization– its severance from nature, indulgence in power and pelf as embodied in Mr. Dalloway, its material pursuit to the utter disregard of art, music, beauty and cravings of human heart, and above all, its systems and institutions, instead of fulfilling the needs of the individual, crush the human spirit and force it into acquiescence and silence– echoing the theme of *silence*. The novel reveals Woolf's genuine civilizational concerns and the urgent need to rectify and arrest its deterioration. Her scathing remarks on the world of London, the microcosm of modern civilization, illustrate this. She equates London with Hell-'a circumscribed mound, eternally burnt, eternally scarred'. The double contextualization of the word– one as the emblem of modern materialistic civilization, London, and the other, the Biblical myth of Inferno– instantly connect the two points of time– the past and the present– which bring out the meaning of the context forcefully and vividly. The unequivocal relation established between Hell and the modern world reflects Woolf's indictment of the latter for its mindless indulgence in materialistic pursuits.

The action of the novel is set partly on the sea and partly on the island. There are beautiful sights and natural flora and fauna: river, sea, mist, the Sun, rain, sea-gulls, pinnacles, smoke, hill, gale, etc. The island is beautiful. Behind the crescent of land there was a deep green with distinct hills on either side of valley. On the slope of the right-side hill white houses with brown roofs nestled; mountains with bald heads rose as a pinnacle. There is a river 'that great stream'. Trees are intense. For Woolf, nature is changeless whereas human life changes in the flux of Time: 'Since the time of Elizabeth, nothing has changed there- the river was the same for Elizabethans and now in the 20th century. The waving green had stood there century after century ...while in other parts of the world one town had risen upon the ruins of another town' (250). Seasons of nature change from place to place. Most of the characters in the novel do not understand the mysteries of Nature. They criticize it instead: 'Oh, but we're all agreed by this time that *nature's a mistake. She's either ugly, appallingly uncomfortable, or absolutely terrifying* (110).

In Woolf's aesthetic, the rhythm of Nature assumes central importance. Woolf incorporated her vision of rhythm in the text not only at the linguistic level, but also as part of the central vision of the novel to express the rhythmic tension between chaos and order, silence and speech, transience and eternity, the natural and human world, life and art– the concerns which were extended to her later fiction as well. In the novel, the rhythmical processes of life and the mind are recreated in concrete set of images in the text, particularly of the human body: 'Screening her face she sobbed more steadily than she had yet done, her shoulders *rising and falling* with great regularity' (4); 'Raising herself and sitting up, she too realized Helen's soft body ... *swelling and breaking* in one vast wave' (268); 'She looks at once *up and down, up and down*, as if one were a horse' (278); 'As she walked, they could see her breast *slowly rise and slowly fall*' (338). These utterances illustrate the fact that the sense of rhythm is innate and an integral part of the novel.

Woolf makes abundant use of imagery at the level of discourse as well as thematic level. For instance,'The afternoon was very hot, so hot that the breaking of the waves on the shore sounded like the repeated sigh of some exhausted creature ...' (308). The example could be elaborated by using linguistic terms:

Tenor: the waves breaking on the shore in the afternoon sun
Vehicle: the repeated sigh of some exhausted creature

The heat of the tropical sun in Santa Marina was so high that the waves, instead of energetically and rhythmically breaking on the shore, were sighing repeatedly like some exhausted creature. The tenor and the vehicle are compared on the *grounds* of the energy of the waves being sucked out, and thus, deenervated and in imminent danger of being reduced to the helpless state of stasis, instead of roaring in youthful force. The metaphorical animation of the waves–

'some exhausted creature'– unlike the deceptively naturalistic description, requires figurative interpretation in the context of Rachel's death by heat. Since Rachel's spirit habitually 'kisses the spirit of the sea' (20) and thus, closer to natural forces, she also feels the heat of the tropical sun as in '... her cheeks ... for they were burning hot' (233). By metaphorical extension of meaning, Rachel was also sighing 'like some exhausted creature', thus, her life-energies being drained out and in danger of being in the motionless, life-less state of stasis. It is no wonder then that Rachel dies by the same heat a few pages later (334). The example reveals Woolf's skill and art in integrating even the naturalistic, descriptive details into the central narrative.

Woolf organizes her texts around symbols. Natural elements such as storm, birds and trees acquire symbolic value in their contexts of use. The tree symbol is significant, since it is used to symbolize eternity in contrast to human impermanence: 'She [Rachel] might have walked until ..., had it not been for the interruption of a tree ... It was an ordinary tree, but to her it appeared so strange that it might have been the only tree in the world. ... Having seen a sight that would last her for a lifetime ... the tree once more sank into the ordinary ranks of trees ...' (159-60).However, the significant symbols having a bearing on narrative structure and thematic structure are the sea and waves. They acquire meaning and significance with reference to Rachel's relationship to them in various contexts of use.

To sum up, the discussion above amply justifies the claim that Woolf arguably is one of the modern writers who expresses ecological concerns in her novels seriously.

References:

1. Daiches D. (1942), *Virginia Woolf*, Norfolk, Connecticut.

2. Majumdar, R and McLaurin, A. (eds.), (1975), *Virginia Woolf: The Critical Heritage*, Routledge and Kegan Paul, London and Boston
3. Kostkowska, J. (2013), *Ecocriticism and Women Writers*, Palgrave Macmillan.
4. Woolf, V. (1992 [1915]), *The Voyage Out*, Penguin Books, London.

Treatment of Women and Nature in Khushwant Singh's *Train to Pakistan*

– Janhavi Jadhav

Bio: Janhavi Sanjay Jadhav, studying English Literature and History at B.K. Birla College (Autonomous), Kalyan, is fond of reading novels and doodling. She considers teaching a noble profession and aspires to become a teacher one day.

Abstract: *Train to Pakistan*'s is a celebrated novel by Khushwant Singh based in a fictional village of Mano Majra which presents the pre-and post-partition situations. It is a small village in Punjab, close to the border. In this village, Sikhs form majority of the population followed by Muslims, Hindus and Christians. In the beginning, all of them are portrayed to be living happily, despite of their religious differences. But the advent of independence on 15th August 1947 and the consequent division of Indian sub-continent into two new states results in, what historians infamously dub as, "August Anarchy". People of Mano Majra, too, are caught in maelstrom of unprecedented violence and anarchic situations. Khushwant Singh forms this as the basis of his novel. This study focuses on the patriarchal structure and male domination in the book The Train to Pakistan. Women are shown to be dependent, submissive and obedient. The trauma of partition was immense but compared to men, women had to face more traumatic situations. Khushwant Singh through his book tries to convey the reality of partition and its long term effects on the minds of people. This paper is a humble attempt to explore Train to Pakistan from a feminist perspective and the consequent forms of marginalization of women. It also aims to reevaluate the text in light of current state of affairs.

Keywords: Patriarchy, Feminism, Marginalization, Partition.

Half a century ago Khushwant Singh, wrote in a column, "Why I am an Indian" that he was convinced that in our guaranteed diversity lies our strength as a nation. He states that it is the consciousness of the frontiers (whether religious, linguistic or gender) is what makes us a nation. A lawyer-author-diplomat-historian-editor by profession, Khushwant Singh always spoke his mind and took stands that very few dared to. His most famous work, Train to Pakistan is a powerful and affective novel capturing the cataclysmic events of 1947 and the intimate details of the existence of the village. Creation of border, to divide India to create the new state of Pakistan, affected more than 100 million inhabitants and was dubbed as the Radcliffe Award. It was the biggest exodus in the history of the subcontinent. The homeless migrants lost not only their land and property but it also

shattered friendships, relations and families. People left everything behind, those who survived could never actually recover from the events, they were unfortunate to witness. Since the countries were divided on communal grounds the whole idea of one's identity, culture, language and tradition also stood shaken. Despite tons of statistics which we have of the episode, the grass root level narrative is actually very different. Writers like Khushwant Singh and Urvashi Butalia manage to bring before us the actual consequences of the 'Great Divide.' They capture the real essence of the events by employing tools of 'Realism', a branch of writing in literature which aims at depicting real or verbatim state of affairs in a particular literary work. Realism aims to depict the actualities of life and to focus on the reality and morality of the people and the society.

Mano Majra is a fictional place in the novel where Sikhs and Muslims have lived together in peace for hundreds of years. Then one day, at the beginning of spring, a "ghost train" arrives, a silent, loaded with the bodies of thousands of refugees, bringing the village its first taste of the horrors of the "Great Divide". *Train to Pakistan* is the story of this isolated village that is plunged into the abyss of communalism and religious hatred. It is also the story of a Sikh boy and a Muslim girl whose love endures and eclipses the ravages of war. The author goes on to narrate the gruesome reality of partition and the consequent marginalization of women and children in the village. The author, very realistically, depicts the escalation of events and introduces the village of Mano Majra in the following lines:

> "The summer before, communal riots, precipitated by reports of the proposed division of the country into a Hindu India and a Muslim Pakistan, had broken out in Calcutta, and within a few months the death toll had mounted to several thousand. Muslims said the Hindus had planned and started the killing. According to the Hindus, the Muslims were to blame. The fact is, both sides were killed. Both shot and stabbed and speared and clubbed. Both tortured. Both raped. Hundreds of thousands of Hindus and Sikhs who had lived for centuries on the Northwest Frontier abandoned their homes and fled towards the protection of the predominantly Sikh and Hindu communities in the east.

> They travelled on foot, in bullock carts, crammed into lorries, clinging to the sides and roofs of trains. By the summer of 1947, when the creation of the new state of Pakistan was formally announced, ten million people—Muslims and Hindus and Sikhs—were in flight. By the time the monsoon broke, almost a million of them were dead, and all of northern India was in arms, in terror, or in hiding. The only remaining oases of peace were a scatter of little villages lost in the remote reaches of the frontier. One of these villages was Mano Majra. (Singh 8)

The author paints realistic picture of villages near the border, before and after India was partitioned.

Khushwant Singh depicts multiculturalism, political idealism, communal violence, suffering, misery, partition trauma, humour, greed, hypocrisy, drunkenness, unjust police, customs and bureaucracy, patriarchy, love and sacrifice. He compares the differences of Sikh and Muslim women and the variation in violence they faced throughout the partition. The common men and women were victimized during partition but the women suffered the most. Men had to face violence but women and children on the other hand were molested, raped, beaten up and brutally harassed.

The patriarchal society and male dominance are portrayed through father-daughter, husband-wife and other relationships. Men are the head of the family structure and women have no specific role in day to day life. Men on one hand have high posts like inspector, sub inspector, religious head, etc. and on the other hand women do household chores, taking care of kids, picking out lice. Women do not have any authority in taking decisions of their own lives. All decisions, even major ones and trivial, are taken for them by their father, brother and husband, after marriage. In one instance, Nooran unwillingly goes with her father instead of her love and desire to stay with Juggut Singh at Mano Majra. She has no courage to inform her father about her love with Juggut and desire to stay with him. This lack of courage in Nooran rises from her fear of challenging the norms predetermined for her by the patriarchs.

Males form bulk of characters in the novel. In the book, there are only two female characters who manage to have some room in the novel. They are also not of great importance in the novel. The first is Nooran the object of Juggut's passion and the second is Haseena who is described as an

object of lust for bureaucrat, Hukum Chand. The whole novel is portrayed around male thinking and male needs. A woman thinking in a novel can hardly be considered. Women are portrayed in the novel as "weaker sex." The author, in subtle ways, reflects the social conditions that exist, even today. Six years after Khushwant Singh's death, Capt. Tanya Shergill, a fourth generation military officer, became the first Indian woman 'Parade Adjutant' to lead an all-men contingent on the Republic Day; Gita Gopinath, an Indian-American economist became the First Woman Chief Economist at the International Monetary Fund; similarly we have numerous examples which show us that Indian women have come a long way. But we also have ghastly cases like Nirbhaya Hatyakand and 2019's Hyderabad gang-rape case. Violent crime against women and discrimination at workplace still persists. Cities like Delhi, Kota and Hyderabad are being infamously dubbed as 'unsafe' for women. Indian workforce figures, too, stand in stark contrast to gender equality numbers. Patriarchal philosophy still maintains that household (kitchen to be specific) is the ' true realm ' of a woman and marriage her ultimate fate.

Women in the novel are also portrayed to be lacking their own subjectivity and in any matters concerning them. When they are discussed, it is in the context of their relationships with men. Even Nooran, who is richly described than any other female character in the novel, is defined in contrast with her relation to man, as Juggut's lover and the daughter of the Muslim weaver, Haseena, a Muslim sex-worker, is apparantly the most impuissant female character in the novel, whose thoughts and feelings are reflected only through her client, Hukum Chand's, point of view. Such features of women reinforce the notion that they lack personality. They are acknowledged only in respect with their position to men.

Women are also regarded as objects or vessels for the desires of men. This could be best represented when Jugga in conversation with Iqbal, describes the British women as elusive and unobtainable sexual objects ("*houris*") and calls Indian women "black buffaloes" because of their darker skin tone. The comparison of English women to *houris*, or angels, reinforces the myth that white women have learned through colonial rule. This could be best exemplified from the lines –

"It was not possible to keep Indians off the subject of sex for long. It obsessed their minds. It came out in their art, literature, and religion ... One read it in the advertisements of quacks who proclaimed to possess remedies for barrenness and medicines to induce wombs to yield male children. One heard about it all the time ...

Conversation on any topic—politics, philosophy, sport—soon came down to sex, which everyone enjoyed it with a lot of giggling and hand-slapping." (Singh 67)

Women in the novel are represented just as an object of desire and sex. Apart from this they have nothing of any significance. Nooran is an object Juggut Singh to channelize his sexual energy.

Their scene of love making is described for three long pages. After having sexual intercourse with Nooran, Juggut is only interested in knowing whether she will come tomorrow. This shows how he is obsessed with sex with Nooran. Haseena, a nineteen year old Muslim girl, is used as a sexual object by Hukum Chand. The magistrate has paid for her. The intimate scenes of Juggut and Nooran and Hukum Chand and Haseena are described simultaneously in the plot. This shows that this type of act may be happening at many places at that time. This reinforces the notion of woman as an object of sex.

When men can not prove their masculinity by sexual exploitation or objectification of women, they resort to violence. In fact, the Sikh men in the novel characterize their manhood by their willingness to confront or commit violence. For example, when a group of Sikh soldiers goes to the Gurdwara during a community meeting, a boy leader stands out among them and baits the Sikh male villagers into killing Muslims by saying that their masculinity depends on it. Singh describes the young man as "small in size, slight of build" and "somewhat effeminate." (Singh 92) This depicts that the boy leader is using his military authority to rouse the male villagers into violence, as a means of validating his own manhood.

Kushwant Singh through many incidents gives us details of how men take revenge by abusing women. The village has fallen silent after the murder of Lala Ram. There is fear, horror, wail, blood, noise of dogs barking in the air around Mano Majra as the dacoits pass on street and give open challenges to the men of the village that they will rape women and girls of Mano Majra.

> 'Come!' they yelled. 'Come out, if you have the courage! Come out, if you want your mothers and sisters to be raped! Come out, brave men!' (Singh 13)

Men look towards women as the gateway to fun. They expect women bodily features to please and satisfy their lust. The spearman describes the body of the weaver's daughter as:

"with those large gazelle eyes and the little mango breasts. What is her name?'

The leader turned off the torch and took it from his mouth. 'Nooran,' he said.

'Aho,' the spearman said. 'Nooran. Did you see her at the spring fair? Did you see that tight shirt showing off her breasts and the bells tinkling in her plaits and the swish-swish of silk? Hai!'

'Hai!' the spearman with the bangles cried. 'Hai! Hai!'
'She must give Jugga a good time,' said the gunman who had not yet spoken. 'During the day, she looks so innocent you would think she had not shed her milk teeth.' He sighed. 'But at night, she puts black antimony in her eyes."
(Singh 10)

Author, through the character of Juggut Singh, highlights the thinking of men of those times who are pleased more by white women as they are white and soft like silk than Indian women whom he calls as black buffaloes. He feels that the black women are not beautiful and compares to an animal.

The author highlights that these values are deeply imbibed in our societies. This is true even in today's world, where women are desired to be fair skinned, having thin waist with silky hair. This patriarchal construct, in fact, gave rise to a multi-million-dollar industry of cosmetics and make-up who only rip-off their customers by exploiting this stereotypical construct.

This could be very well observed in the lines of Juggut Singh, who says -

"Wah, Babuji – great. You must have had lots of fun. The memsahibs are like houris from paradise – white and soft,

like silk. All we have here are black buffaloes."
(Singh 113)

Javaid Iqbal and Eti Sharma in paper "Khushwant's Train to Pakistan: A Critique of the Impact and Ugliness of Partition" explore the same narrative in detail. They correctly observe:

"Ladies had an exceptionally tricky or defenseless position amid the savage occasions; they were assaulted or snatched by the men of the two countries so as to demonstrate their manliness and the effeminacy of the other network. Numerous young ladies and wedded ladies were left to their destiny after they were assaulted. These ladies were not acknowledged by their families as they were viewed as disfavored and carried on with the life of the living dead. The story recommends how Partition cost human lives, executing people as well as their family ties and social connections." [2]

A sub inspector in 'Train to Pakistan' arranges a virgin girl, Haseena for the magistrate, Hukum Chand for him to enjoy. Haseena dances on a love song innocently as she is frightened to deny the lustful behavior of the magistrate, Hukum Chand. An old woman scolds her go near Hukum Chand and refers to him as "Government" This shows how men when bestowed with even a little power will not stop there and go on to exploit it. Her chastity has no value of men. Her agony is shown in lines-

"Hukum Chand put his arm around her waist.

'You sing well.'

The girl gaped wide-eyed at her companions.

'The Government is talking to you. Why don't you answer him?' scolded the old woman.

'Government, the girl is young and very shy. She will learn,' she exclaimed. Haseena was pushed forcefully to her exploitation for pleasing Hukum Chand. Haseena became a prostitute for Hukum Chand day by day." (Singh 23)

Nature is usually regarded as something to be exploited by human-beings. In the same manner, the patriarchal society regards women as "natural resource, as an asset to be owned and harnessed, harvested and mined, with no fellow-feeling for her depletion and no responsibility for her conservation or replenishment" [3]. In this novel, Hukum Chand, a corrupted district magistrate, exploits and demeans a teenage girl named Haseena Begum.

His maltreatment of the teenage girl can be discerned by eco-feminists who argue that, "Patriarchal society's values and beliefs have resulted in the oppression of both women and nature. It ignores women's work, knowledge and situatedness (her immediate location in nature, where the relationship with the environment is far more intimate than that of a man)."

The girl is not at all beautiful, but "young and unexploited" (Singh 23) like the virgin nature, that can attract men. Hukum Chand is no exception. Haseena may be younger than his daughter, yet that does not bother him at all. He exploits his authority. Being a dominant member of the patriarchal society, he is just concerned with the female body that he looks forward to exploit. Earth as well as virgin girls are meant to be exploited by men. This is exemplified by the author in lines-

"[H]er breasts barely filled her bodice. They could not have known the touch of a male hand". She is no more than a passive sporting tool to him. Her helplessness is articulated even in her song where she compares her to

a moth that "loves the flame" and succumbs to death."
(Singh 23)

Nature seems to counteract when a ghost train, full of
dead bodies of Hindus, arrives from Pakistan.

All day long the villagers of Mano Majra dubiously wait
to know what the train has transported from Pakistan:
they stand on the roofs to peek at what is happening at the
railway station, women forget to cook food, hungry
children cry out for food yet women do not light the
hearts, and men do not tend their cattle. But they do not
know anything until nature reveals the heinous deed for
them.

At night, Sikh soldiers slyly try to burn the corpses in
order to conceal any knowledge of the brutal killing,
violence, rape, and destruction from the villagers. Nature,
however, is portrayed to be the agent of truth and it
reveals that-

"A soft breeze began to blow towards the village. It
bought the smell of burning kerosene, then wood. And
then — a faint acrid smell of searing flesh. The village
was stilled in a deathly silence. No one asked anyone
what the odour was. They all knew.

They had known it all the time." (Singh 55)

Nature also revolts against the gruesome endeavor of
wiping out traumatic history of partition by rain that
extinguishes the fire and exposes "a hundred yards of
charred corpses" (Singh 60).

Later on in the novel, an excessive rain mourns for the
deportation of the Muslims from the village of Mano
Majra. The villagers can no longer bear the chaotic
situation. Thus, nature is portrayed by the author to be
karmic in its feature. It could be seen in the line:

"rise more and drown the whole of Mano Majra along with them, their women, children, and cattle — provided it also drowned Malli, his gang, his refugees, and soldiers". (Singh 88)

Nature responses to this urge and the water level of the river rises and the stream becomes "a menacing and tumultuous spread of muddy down" (Singh 88). Within two days the Sutlej turns into terrifying sight. It seems that the river is rebelling against all cruelty and inhumanity. The river yields thousands of corpses of men, women, babies, bulls, horses. From the side of the river, the people hear human voices crying out for help. The water of the river is rising higher. The overwhelming wounds of partition are revealed by author in the lines –

"There were many others coming down the river like logs hewn on the mountains and cast into streams to be carried down to the plains. A few passed through the middle of the arches and sped onward faster. Others bumped into the piers and turned over to show their wounds till the current turned them over again. Some were without limbs, some had their bellies torn open, many women's breasts were slashed. They floated down the sunlit river, bobbing up and down. Overhead hung the kites and vultures" (Singh 90)

Khushwant Singh, like a true humanist, has always been vocal against the fanaticism and hypocrisy of religion and faith. In majority of his works, he has been critical of all religions, per say. He believes it is because of religion events of partition unfolded so horribly wrong – victimizing thousands of people (mostly women and children). In Train to Pakistan, we get a deep insight into Khushwant Singh's moral and philosophical viewpoint. He is quite Maxist in his view regarding religion being just a facade. Like Marx, he believes that religion too has adopted the capitalist notion of ripping of people to earn profits and lost its original purpose. He has also been criticized numerous times for employing a vulgar language in his narration. This could be seen in lines:

"India is constipated with a lot of humbug. Take religion. For the Hindu, it means little besides caste and cow-protection. For the Muslim, circumcision and kosher meat. For the Sikh, long hair and hatred of the Muslim. For the Christian, Hinduism with a sola topee. For the Parsi, fire-worship and feeding vultures. Ethics, which should be the kernel of a religious code, has been carefully removed. Take philosophy, about which there is so much hoo-ha. It is just muddle-headedness masquerading as mysticism. And Yoga, particularly Yoga, that excellent earner of dollars! Stand on your head. Sit cross-legged and tickle your navel with your nose. Have perfect control over the senses. Make women come till they cry 'Enough!' and you can say 'Next, please' without opening your eyes. And all the mumbo-jumbo of reincarnation. Man into ox into ape into beetle into eight million four hundred thousand kinds of animate things. Proof? We do not go in for such pedestrian pastimes as proof! That is Western. We are of the mysterious East. No proof, just faith. No reason, just faith." (Singh 105)

The death of Jugga is a perfect example of the absurdity of fate. He single-handedly saves the Mano Majra Muslims. His character evolves, since the beginning of the novel, Jugga is portrayed in bad light; as a villian in the eye of whole village. But when time comes he takes his stand against religious persecution and proves to be a moral man. In the end, the angry mob ties a thick rope on top of the two towers to strangle Muslims who were escaping off to Pakistan on top of the train. But Jugga determined to save them takes on the task of cutting the rope. His struggle is exemplified in lines- "He went at it with the knife, and then with his teeth. The engine was almost on him.

There was a volley of shots. The man shivered and collapsed. The rope snapped in the centre as he fell. The train went over him, and went on to Pakistan." (Singh 111)

Khushwant Singh, through Jugga's sacrifice, reminds us all that humanity will always win; that there will always be men who will remind us what it is to be human and to rise above our petty differences of caste, race, religion, creed and gender.

Conclusion:

On a concluding note, reading Train to Pakistan is not for weak hearted, it is a gut-wrenching experience. Khushwat Singh in his novel Train to Pakistan did not try to open old wounds but rather stitch them. He believes that humanity will always rise above our petty differences. The novel subtly recounts women's experiences who haggle through multiple identities in order to survive the horrendous episodes of partition. Through this literary marvel Khushwant Singh reminds us that only kindness, in the end, can be repaid with kindness. It would not be wrong to conclude that through this novel, Khushwant Singh renders how patriarchal, conservative-national codes and practices have been normalized in India since the 'Great Divide' and revamped with the horrors of partition. He manages to do so by unfolding the plot through eyes of different characters, belonging to different generations, different genders and different religions and contrasting their experiences and ideologies with each other. He manages to give insight into the complexities of women and their relationships in this patriarchal society and urges that it is high time we address them. With help of this novel, it would be apt to conclude that Khushwant Singh is a progressive writer and he continues to remind us that partition of 1947 was not a mere division of land, rather a division of friends, hearts, families, souls and most of all 'humanity'; and that it was the ordained forces of masculinist-nationalism and innate hatred for the 'other' which provoked the masses to inflict such wounds, on both men and women, Indian and Pakistani, Hindu and Sikh, that even after 73-long years they are yet to heal.

Works Cited

1. Khushwant, Singh. Train to Pakistan. New York: Grove Press, 1961. Print.

2. Iqbal, Javad, and Eti Sharma. "Khushwant's Train to Pakistan: A Critique of the Impact and Ugliness of Partition." IJIRT Journal, vol. 6, no. 1, June 2019.

3. Dinnerstein, Dorothy. The Mermaid and the Minotaur: Sexual Arrangements and Human Malaise. New York: Harper & Row, 1976. Print.

4. Nayar, Pramod. Contemporary Literary and Cultural Theory: From Structuralism to Ecocriticism. Pearson, 2010.

Environmental Activism and Eco-Fiction

- Dr. Lakshmi Muthukumar

Bio: Dr. Lakshmi Muthukumar heads the department of English at the South Indian Education Society's College of Arts, Science and Commerce, Sion West, Mumbai. She has 25 years of experience in teaching undergraduate students language and literature. She also teaches postgraduate students at the National College as a visiting faculty and is a registered guide for Ph.D. Her areas of interest include language studies, gender studies and creative writing.

Abstract:

This paper attempts to present eco-fiction as a genre that offers great potential for amateur writers of fiction. It also tries to spell out its salient features. It seeks to clarify questions such as, "Is eco-fiction simply fiction set in nature?" and "What is the rubric for writing such a work?"Another objective of the presentation is to make budding writers aware of the scope such fiction offers. Last, but not the least, the paper also tries to make a case for eco-fiction to be included in the syllabi of literature programmes that teach papers in Popular Culture or World Literature not only as samples of how creative artists might become inspirational change makers but also of how young minds might be made aware of the challenges posed by climate change for humanity.

Keywords: Green fiction, Environmental consciousness raising and Cli-Fi

English Literature courses in India focus largely on British Literature, Indian Literature in English and American Literature in a genre-based format while also acquainting students with critical tools to appreciate these literary works. These critiques include feminist, modernist and postmodern interpretations. While learners who study feminism are subjected to some consciousness-raising when it comes to gender, the environmental awareness that is so crucial to our times takes a backseat. In what can only be termed as an exercise in tokenism, courses on literature and gender sometimes include a segment on Eco-feminism. This does not even come close to making the youth aware of the challenges that humans pose to the environment today, let alone focus serious attention on issues such as global warming and seasonal change.

One of the objectives of this paper is to recommend that syllabi of literature programmes include a course on Eco-Fiction. This will not only make the learners aware of the dangers that the environment is beset with today but also give them a glimpse into world literatures written in English in various forms such as Poetry for Climate change, Cli-Fi or Green Fiction or Eco-Fiction and even graphic novels such as *The Rime of the Modern Mariner* by Nick Hayes. Written in 2010, this graphic novel is a take-off on Coleridge's famous poem "The Rime of the Ancient Mariner" and is an excellent example of graphic eco-fiction. It is an engaging Eco Fable set in the cesspool of the North Atlantic Garbage Patch, thus adding another dimension to Eco-Fiction. Such an innovative course could be titled as a paper on World Literature and could have environmental awareness as one of its objectives. Another important objective of such a course could be to introduce learners to literatures written in English in parts of the world other than the West.

Another suggestion that will instill environmental consciousness raising and awareness amongst young learners is to offer creative writing programmes with a focus on green fiction. That way students not just from the Humanities, but also from Life Sciences such as Biology, Botany, Zoology, Microbiology and Biochemistry with a yen to tell a tale may be taught how to do just that by marrying their knowledge of species of flora and fauna that are going extinct with a fictive account of how the human race is responsible for such extinction. In order to teach such a course, it is necessary to understand what exactly Eco-Fiction is and what would constitute a rubric for writing such fiction. Such courses will also encourage a healthy interaction between students of the Humanities and Life Sciences.

The term "Eco-Fiction", became prevalent from the 1970s and is used to refer to a branch of literature that encompasses nature-oriented works of fiction. Such fiction focuses on both non-human as well as environment-oriented work that gives perspectives on the impact of humans on nature. Nomenclature of this kind of fiction is varied and ranges from terms such as environmental fiction, nature-oriented fiction, Cli-Fi to Green Fiction. According to Jonathan Levin, the term "Eco-Fiction" emerged soon after ecology took hold as a popular scientific paradigm and a broad cultural attitude in the 1960s and 1970s. Eco-fiction is an elastic term, capacious enough to accommodate a variety of fictional works that address the relationship between natural settings and the human communities that dwell within.

In order to understand how Eco-Fiction differs from fiction that simply has a natural setting, it is necessary to list its salient features or characteristics. Creating such a list is necessary even from the point of view of providing a rubric for budding writers of fiction who wish to try their hand at Eco-Fiction as an upcoming genre. Internationally, there are several writers who are producing this kind of fiction. However, in India, such fiction has only been attempted by a few. In the 1970s Zai Whitaker and in 1991, Perumal Murugan who wrote such a novel in Tamil entitled *Eru Veyyil*(Translated as *Rising Heat*) are some of the names that immediately come to mind. The twenty first century has seen novelists such as Amitav Ghosh whose novels such as *The Ibis Trilogy*, especially *The Hungry Tide* and *Gun Island* (his most recent work) popularized the form among readers while also generating environmental activism through his non-fiction such as *The Great Estrangement*. Several of Amitav Ghosh's novels address environmental concerns with a fierce urgency that is usually witnessed only among environmental activists. The novels showcase the precarious predicament of people whose lives have been irrevocably affected by the repercussions of climate change. Apart from Amitav Ghosh, another writer who has emerged on the scene is Rajat Chauduri whose novel *The Butterfly Effect* has created ripples on the literary scene.

There are three salient features of Eco-Fiction that can be identified. Firstly, the nonhuman environment is present not merely as a framing device but as a presence that begins to suggest that human history is implicated in natural history.

Secondly, the human interest is not understood to be the only legitimate interest. Thirdly, human accountability to the environment should be part of the text's ethical orientation. Last, but not least, some sense of the environment as a process rather than as a constant or given is usually implicit in a work of Eco-Fiction.

Mike Vasey has laid down some principles that are to be followed by writers of such fiction. These include two major ones. Such stories are usually set in fictional landscapes that capture the essence of natural ecosystems. Also, the story necessarily takes the reader into the natural world and brings it alive. This is beautifully evidenced in Barbara Kingsolver's novel *Flight Behaviour*. This novel revolves around a new winter habitat for monarch butterflies after their traditional habitat is destroyed by flooding due to climate change. Kingsolver skillfully blends science with fiction by addressing climate change through the eyes of a woman whose small world is shaken by a bizarre natural event. The protagonist Dellarobia Turnbow reaches the mountains for a rendezvous with a man only to discover a vast population of monarch butterflies. The unseasonal arrival of these butterflies signifies a miracle to the locals while to the scientific community, it portends an ecological disaster. With great felicity and empathic engagement Kingsolver portrays the implications of climate change on the unsuspecting ecology.

There are quite a few writers of Eco-Fiction who are making the scene lively and engaging such as the American authors Ann Pancake and the Australian novelist, James Bradley. Ann Pancake's novel, *Strange as this Weather* has been, is a novel set in the midst of a town witnessing a coal boom. The novelist poignantly brings out the effects of the mountaintop removal by strip mining that destroys the surrounding land. Pancake, who hails from West Virginia, writes with great authenticity using testimonials of locals who have actually lived through mountaintop removal mining. Place is a major character in this novel and as the character Lace says, "Stay in their way-that's the only language they can hear." This quote brings out the desperate measures that the local people have to resort to in order to ensure that their rights are protected and their voices heard.

Patricia D. Netzley classifies novels that belong to the genre of Eco-Fiction into three categories. The first category includes works that portray the environmental movement and/or environmental activism, the second category consists of works that depict a conflict over an environmental issue while also expressing the author's beliefs and the third category consists of works that feature an environmental apocalypse. This classification will also help researchers theorize such works even as it assists in embedding fiction within the broader arena of environmental fiction as a type of environmental activism because it leads to environmental awareness and consciousness-raising.

It is precisely for this reason that one is building a case for such fiction to be encouraged at the undergraduate level through courses in creative writing with an emphasis on Eco-Fiction. Literature programmes at the undergraduate level can also include Eco-Fiction as a term that can be taught to their learners just as they teach terms such as Gothic fiction or the Graphic novel. The times we live in are grim if one were to mull over environmental crises looming large. Therefore, including such fiction in our literature courses will encourage useful discussions in class and ensure that students think and read about issues such as global warming and non-seasonal migration that adversely impact the ecology.

References:

1. Dwyer, Jim (2010). *Where the Wild Books are: A Field Guide to Eco Fiction*. University of Nevada Press.

2. Murphy, Patrick D. (2000). *Further Afield in the Study of Nature-Oriented Literature*. Charlottesville: University Press of Virginia.

3. Navarre, Gabriel (1980). *Earthworks: Ten Years on the Environmental Front*. San Francisco: Friends of the Earth. pp. 218–219.

4. Netzley, Patricia (1991). *Environmental Literature: An Encyclopedia of Works, Authors and Themes*. Santa Barbara, CA: ABC-Clio. P. 78.

5. Vasey, Mike (February 20, 1996). *Bioregional Studies - Correspondence with Jim Dwyer*.

The Self, Community and Nature: An Ecocritical Reading of Kaveri Nambisan's *The Scent of Pepper*

- Dr. Nisha Nambiar

Bio: Dr. Nisha Nambiar is an Assistant Professor of English at Krishna Menon Memorial Government Women's College, Pallikunnu, Kannur, Kerala.

Abstract:
This article undertakes to examine in Kaveri Nambisan's novel *The Scent of Pepper*, the relationship between humanity and the natural world of the Kodavas and recommends greater inclusion and evaluation. The novelist reiterates that the connections with nature help us strengthen our sense of self and find our meaning in life as well as combat feelings of anxiety and meaninglessness. The text becomes a space wherein the identity of the Kodavas and their racial and ethnic history gets inscribed and further could also be seen as an attempt made by the novelist to preserve their ethnicity on the onslaught of migration and westernisation. The paper will stress upon the crystallisation of this unique relationship between the Kodava community and nature and specifically the intimating bonding of the female protagonist and her region.

Keywords: Exploring selfhood, bonding between man and nature, woman as nurturer, preserving ecology

This article undertakes to examine Kaveri Nambisan's novel *The Scent of Pepper*, from the perspective of ecocriticism by exploring the ecological consciousness represented and interwoven in the characters, setting and plot of the novel. The theoretical framework of ecocriticism is illustrated in literature by grounding the study of literature in the earth that surrounds and sustains us. The ecocritical stance reconnects literary study to both the processes and the problems inherent in living on this earth, focusing our attention anew on the complex and intrinsic relationships among self, society, nature, and text.

Pepper probes into the relationship between humanity and the natural world of the Kodavas and recommends greater inclusion and evaluation. The novelist reiterates that the connections with nature help us strengthen our sense of self and find our meaning in life as well as combat feelings of anxiety and meaninglessness. The text becomes a space wherein the identity of the Kodavas and their racial and ethnic history gets inscribed and further could also be seen as an attempt made by the novelist to preserve their ethnicity on the onslaught of migration and westernisation. In doing so it attempts to bring to the fore how the region of Kodagu with its distinct culture encompassing its myths, customs and beliefs, structures her narrative and examines how far the author has been successful in artistically realising it.

Ecocritical and feminist discourses have strongly engaged for the case that women are closer to nature and this fact has been woven into the tapestry of literature and art. Though one can trace this closeness in the female protagonist of *Pepper*, on no grounds does it claim that men are distanced from it. The paper will stress upon the crytallisation of the unique relationship between the Kodava community and nature, laying special emphasis on the intimate bonding of the female protagonist and her region.

A very interesting fact about Kaveri Nambisan's personality is that despite having acquired her medical degree and then her surgical training in England, she has dedicated herself to working in the rural areas of India. Nambisan's hands-on experience of the life of the poor in a rural community has seeped into her writing to impart a realistic note to it. She began her literary career by writing stories under the name Kavery Bhatt for the now defunct children's magazine *Target* in the 1980s and her debut novel, *The Truth (Almost) About Bharat (*1991). The cross-country journey of Bharat, a medico-student, on his motor bike through the cultural contours of India forms the core of the novel. Enroute to Kerala, he passes through Mysore and stays in Kodagu–a place he loves with its clustered bamboo groves, coffee estates, and pepper creepers. Her novels, *Mango-Coloured Fish (2000) and On Wings of Butterflies (2002)* narrate her experiences with women who are physically, mentally and psychologically exploited by society. the experiences in her surgical life are best reflected in the character of Nalli in *The Hills of Angheri* (2005). The poverty and squalor of the slums and the apathy felt by the middle class towards the migrant labourers on whom they depend for their sustenance have been vividly etched in her work, *The Story That Must Not Be Told* (2010).

Pepper narrates the story of a feudal family in Athur village, the Kaleyanda, headed by the pattedara, Rao Bahadur. He had sent two of his sons to England and one to Madras for their education. When Baliyanna graduated as a veterinary surgeon from Madras with "a degree that even the British respect", Rao Bahadur decided to move from the family's Iyn House. He bought a "sprawling house, one hundred and twelve acres of newly-planted coffee and five thousand battis of land in Athur" (10). As widow remarriage was permitted among the Kodavas, Nanji, the young widow of the Kongeitra clan is married to Baliyanna, a popular vet among the British planters settled in Kodagu. On the very first day, the tough Nanji decides that she would make her home into a strong fortress and takes charge of the sprawling house in Athur. Having tided resolutely through thirteen pregnancies, and braving her way through the travails of life, she remains steadfast and indispensable to her home. By the end of the novel, Nanji is an old lady with only her favourite son Subbu for company.

The annexation of Kodagu in 1834 by the British set the stage for the entry of the British planters who were searching for an alternative as their plantations in Ceylon were destroyed by the borer pest. They discovered that Coorg with its black moist soil and plenty of shade would be the most ideal for the cultivation of coffee and that the natives, inspite of all their ignorance were wise when it comes to cultivation. Captivated by the extensive coffee plantations and lured by the prospects of a flourishing coffee trade, the British settled down in Coorg. The borer and the leaf-rot that had first appeared in Ceylon, crept along the ghats and gradually invaded Kodagu. With less than fifty British planters in Kodagu who paid him promptly, Baliyanna the vet "led a life of genteel poverty" (101). Their personal disgruntlement at the dwindling prices of coffee and the rising hostility of the natives for independence were now making it obvious to the British that their departure from the land was inevitable. As waves of nationalism swept across the breadth of the country, the Kodavas too were not spared. While majority of the Kodavas were busy imbibing an alien culture, a few like Subbu and his friends join the Congress.

The detailed descriptions of the landscape, the people, their myths and legends, their customs and traditional beliefs blend seamlessly with that of Nature. Myths form an integral part of the local culture and are fraught with the knowledge of the region's history, ecology and religious beliefs. One notices that the myths illustrated in *Pepper* are never a direct explanation of the subject matter but reflect "the fullness of life itself from which the myth is born" (Malinowski 198). The exact origins of the Kodavas are shrouded in mystery and no definitive research has ascertained this fact. In *Pepper*, the myths regarding the origin of the Kodavas include the names of actual kings and civilisations drawn from history. Nambisan describes the race to be the descendants of the troops of Alexander who settled down in "the heavenly hill country." Another myth stated is that they were descendants of the "nobility whose blood stayed red for six hours after death" and to these clans belonged the most beautiful women that a man had to slay nine suitors before he won his bride (*Pepper* 168). Such myths have been incorporated into their marriage rituals, as one is made to understand from the novel, wherein the groom cuts down nine banana trees with his odikkathi before claiming his bride. Religious myths mentioned include the divine origin of the river Kaveri and other localised myths associated with the Forests of Kolabenna. Nambisan claims that the Kodavas adopted their distinct style of wearing their saris "from the toddy-tapping Kudiya women who swung back the pleats when they climbed the panne tree" (*Pepper* 26). This practice has evolved over the years for very practical reasons as it allows the hands to be free for household work and for transplanting rice in the fields.

In *Pepper*, the region is realistically rendered through its verdant valleys, fast flowing streams, paddy fields, coffee bushes, cardamom and pepper plantations and the unfailing rains that assure them of a bountiful produce. The isolation of the region located amidst thick jungles and mountain ranges contributes to the distinctive mode of life and culture of the Kodavas. The novel roughly pans the period from 1850s to 1960s which the reader is able to deduce from the influx of the British planters to Kodagu, the fall of the prices of coffee due to the extension of cultivation in Brazil, the nationalist movement, the visit of Gandhi and the merger of Kodagu. However, the passage of time in the novel is indicated through the cycle of seasons, the cultivation of paddy and coffee and the onset of festivals.

Nambisan presents the Kodavas to be a handsome, brave and warrior like race. Its distinguished martial tradition continues even today with many young Kodavas enlisting themselves as soldiers. *Pepper* clearly substantiates this: 'We're a physically strong race, athletic and skilled in arms [....] [and] it is said that you can roam the length and breadth of the country and never find as unerring a shot as the best among us' [....] 'Tiger skins and bison heads grace our homes. Any woman worth her man has a handful of tiger-claw ornaments to choose from. Our children cut their first teeth on the meat of bison, boar, wildfowl and rabbit ...' (64)

The novelist redefines the stereotype of bravery normally associated with men and succeeds in creating an arena where the women are as capable of displaying physical bravery as the men. Every Kodava family has a fund of stories citing the valour of their women. Nambisan's Nanji came from a family where the women were industrious without the lazy habits of men and they toiled in the fields along with their workers. She discovered from her grandma Neelakki, who had learnt to shoot when she was young, that as a woman one could be strong or weak as one wished. Nambisan's description of Nanji is as follows: Her toughness had mingled with the mud with which the walls were built and the varnish that coated the beams; it had blended into the cowdung wash on the floors and split into the paddy fields and the soft soil beneath the coffee bushes. You could taste her determination in the sweetness of the oranges, and the charm of her hospitality in the flowers that grew around the house. (187)

Whether she is occupied with the enormous task of feeding her family and servants or involved in sowing, transplanting seeds and looking at errant leaves of the coffee plant, Nanji efficiently manages her responsibilities with ease.

Nevertheless, Nambisan points out that the tragedy of this fierce and iron-willed people is that they fall prey to the disease endemic to the area. Nanji witnessed the inevitable signs of depression in her own husband when he indulged in long sessions of loneliness. It was this very malady which compelled her uncles, her brother-in law and many other men of Kodagu to commit suicide. Later on in the novel, her son Subbu succumbs to this "insidious, unrelenting awareness of the futility of existence" (259). In an e-mail message, the novelist (being a doctor) identifies this malady called Endogenous Depression to be common in Coorg, a depression without an obvious traceable cause (7 Oct. 2011). In the past, this loneliness was created to a large extent by Nature itself. The sprawling house of a clan was separated from its neighbours by vast stretches of hills and jungles. The loneliness experienced, especially by the men folk could account for the malady mentioned above (Prabhakaran 87). Unlike them, the women who constantly engaged in the activities of the large household along with the other women of the joint family were strong and shouldered responsibility. As rightly evaluated by the noted Malayalam writer, N. Prabhakaran in his travelogue *Kodagu Kurippukal*, while the women bravely confront the hardships and obstacles of life, at a particular stage of their lives most of the men folk become alcoholics and depressive by nature (87). Even when the house was thronging with relatives, Baliyanna "sat on the porch all day, gazing at the swaying areca palms, while the constant chatter of female voices and the outrageous revelry of innumerable children passed by him like the gusts of wind"(*Pepper* 95). The changes she noticed in her husband made Nanji willingly take up the responsibility of the house and the fields. The only comfort he derived was from alcohol which gave him "the passive contentment of partial living" (98).

Liquor and pork which form the most popular food items of the Kodavas are also made as offerings to their gods. Their martial nature coupled with their love for hunting could account for their "strong carnivorous appetite" (*Pepper* 36). Kodavas are presented in *Pepper* as food lovers and elaborate references to their cuisine are generously strewn into the narrative. Nambisan comments: "'Whatever a Kodava does or does not do, he loves to eat like a king' "(*Pepper* 111). As a people who revelled in their hospitality, there was never a dearth of food lavished on guests. Nanji fed her guests who came in large numbers from the neighbouring villages to the Kaleyanda house. She willingly looks after her brother-in-law, the invalid Appachu till his last days.

Descriptions of the calendar festivals and harvest festivals help capture the solidarity and individuality of the community while emphasising the role that nature plays in this singular relationship. While Kaveri Sankramana celebrates the birth of the river Kaveri, Kailpodh (festival of arms) and Puthari are associated with paddy cultivation. The most significant among all the celebrations in Kodagu is the harvest festival called *Puthari*. The rites performed at the harvest festival, directly or indirectly stresses the great value of rice to the Kodavas (Srinivas, *Religion* 232). On the auspicious Puthari full moon night, the family with all their workers wend their way into the paddy fields and cut the first ripe sheaves of paddy to the cries of 'Poli, poli, poli deva...'("increase, increase O God"). The sheaves were then tied to their doors and bedposts and the ancestors were propitiated (*Pepper* 109). After the culmination of the games and dances, all the males cooperate in the collective hunt that is held after the Kailpodh and Puthari festivals. The share of the hunt is distributed as in the song sung by the hunters soaked in toddy:

Come, oh wild boar ...
My knife is sharp for you.

Your thighs are for me,
Your breasts for my mates.
A cut for the Yeravas,
Your head for the dogs.
Come, oh wild boar.... (*Pepper* 135)

Songs such as the one quoted above are very popular in Kodagu and Nambisan claims to have grown listening to them (email). Srinivas remarks that Kodava custom of hunting demanded that "a man who shoots at an animal must not only hit it, but must draw blood as well" and punishment is meted out on failure to do so (*Religion* 240). Subbu's punishment for missing the deer is a case in point in the novel (134). Another interesting practice connected to hunting was the mock wedding performed to honour someone who had slain a tiger (*"nari mangala")*. When the Puthari festivities were over, the Kodavas would get down to serious business of paddy selling and coffee picking. Every clan participated in the annual caravan that proceeded to Malabar and the return of the men with money in their purses signalled the onset of festivities and marriages. When coffee replaced rice, as illustrated in the novel, the caravans loaded with coffee beans set out for Mangalore.

Besides the festivals mentioned above, births, deaths and marriages are also occasions when ritual performances become mandatory. The ritual idiom integrated into *Pepper* sheds light on their unique customs and traditions.

A significant fact to be noted in connection with all the rituals in Kodagu is that the ancestors are placed along with or even above their gods. Nanji believed that the spirits of their ancestors resided in the clouds blessing their lands with bountiful rains. This ethnic race worships their local cobra-deity, Lord Iguthappa, who is prayed to for rain and prosperity. Nambisan's knowledge of the superstitions and beliefs of the Kodavas have been knitted into the novel, a few of which are listed here – white and red flowers are placed on the idol of the deity in a temple and it was believed that if the white flower falls first it was a good omen and marriages could be solemnised (180), rains falling vertically down or slanting were indications of the temperament of their ancestors (169) and when Baliyanna plucks out the tooth of his children, he puts it in a pellet of cow dung and threw them on the thatched roof of the house "to guarantee a strong new successor to the evicted tooth" (98).

Thus it becomes apparent that the rituals and beliefs in *Pepper* act "as a form of cultural shorthand" (Fetterman 29) in providing a framework to convey an essence of a culture.

On closer examination one finds that the basic doctrine saturating her text has been drawn from the Transcendentalist philosophy and the *Bhagavad Gita*. The Western intellectual insights gained during her stay in England have been braided together with the philosophy of the *Gita* into an Indian mode of narration. In an interview, Nambisan acknowledges that Gandhi and Thoreau have greatly influenced her as a writer and in her medical profession (Writing with the Scalpel). It is a known fact that Emerson and Thoreau were palpably influenced by the deep knowledge of the Eastern texts, particularly the enduring value of the *Bhagavad Gita*. The transcendentalists were mainly opposed to the rigid rationalism, social conformity and materialism that they found increasingly dominant in American life. Their new outlook emphasized the ethics of individualism – of self trust, self sufficiency and self reliance and a return to nature. In place of the formal or doctrinal religion, they advocated a faith in the 'spirit' or the 'soul' in which both humanity and the cosmos participate.

In *Pepper*, Nambisan espouses the concept of *dharma* which is to a large extent accomplished through the character of Nanji. As long as one's conduct is in conformity with his essential nature it gives him a rootedness, the very essence of an individual. It is a quality of spiritual being, a quality of internal realisation. Nanji is, in a sense, striving for realising her selfhood and succeeds in her endeavour. She believes in work and follows the dictum of the *Gita* that 'Work is worship' and has "no time for frivolous feminine pastimes, like singing or embroidery, that seemed to engage other women" (*Pepper*24). In his essay, "Self Reliance", Emerson emphasises on work which he considers is necessary to reinforce oneself (32). Nanji believes that her *dharma* lies is in managing her home and caring for her husband and children, working in the fields and living truly and honestly as a Kodavathi. In her world, Nanji finds the scope for the expression of her life and hence the social routine never becomes a bondage. Instead of rejecting her duties and relationships, she remains with her family till the end of her days. Her unity with the world around her is achieved through her spontaneity of love and unselfish work. Nambisan never presents her as the "passive and suffering" woman who fails to find a voice for herself. Nor is she presented as one who overthrows existing values and systems to build a world of her own. Nanji celebrates her womanhood and cherishes it. This is evident in her discourse on women to Neelu, her grandchild: "We are all of us both delicate and strong.... Look– men can be clay in our hands and every woman knows it. But we must never misuse that power. Nor should we exist only for them." (251). She faces the death of her children as if it were "a physical battering" and keeps herself occupied with the rituals of mourning. The signs of depression she noticed in her husband made Nanji willingly take up the responsibility of the house and the fields. She lets her husband go to the gypsy women hoping he would find solace there and has absolute faith in him regarding his friendship with Clara. This is not the callousness of a woman or her defeatism but it is her capacity for tolerance that shows her strength as an individual in the face of adversities. Her pragmatic approach to life springs from her "instinctive dislike for changes" and resistance "to those that did not spring out of her tenets" (*Pepper* 22). Nanji realises the only honourable way is to rely on oneself (*Pepper* 103). This explicitly underscores Emerson's thesis statement on self-reliance: "Trust thyself: every heart vibrates to that iron string" (28). It is only when the individual commemorates his integrity that he discovers the oneness with the region and transcends it to become a part of the universe at large.

The novel underscores the Emersonian conviction that envy is ignorance and imitation of any sort is suicidal to one's individuality (28). On similar lines, Thoreau remarks:" Let everyone mind their own business, and endeavour to be what he was made" (215). Both Emerson and Thoreau stress the need for every individual to avoid conformity and false consistency, and follow his or her own instincts and ideas. The true children of Kodagu– the Yeravas along with the Kurubas who roamed the hills to collect wild honey and the Kudiyas who climbed the palm trees and tapped toddy, remain ingrained in their own identities and never ape the higher class Kodavas. In contrast, Nambisan presents the few upper class Kodavas who having assimilated the coloniser's mentality, consider themselves to be culturally superior and rubbished their cultural values. Little do they realise that "a foolish consistency is the hobglobin of little minds" (Emerson 34). Just as Kodagu became Coorg, names of estates like Kodanad, Thenupare and Kurudarahalli are changed to Glenview, Windermere and Balmoral respectively. Baliyanna speaks of the Alsatians and Labradors as fashionable pets of the upper class anglicized Kodavas, which were useless for hunting unlike the kani, rajapalyam and chippiparai that belonged to the pure hunter breed of Kodagu. The hibiscus, kanakambara, savanthige and sampige that grew wild in their gardens were pulled down and poppies, asters and snapdragons were planted with meticulous precision.

Pepper expresses its strong belief in pantheism which enforces the idea of the sacredness of nature and considers the cosmos as the all encompassing. Nanji's forte, says Nambisan, was her affection "that extended not just to everyone, but for everything that lived" (42). When Clara asks Baliyanna if he would miss her when the British left India, he gives a cryptic response: 'You and I, we treat sick animals and people without knowing which lives are more precious. This is a blessing because we will try to save them all. Sometimes you see a special appeal in a sheep, horse, cow or– a person, and it hits you. I– will miss you when you go.' (80)

It is the reply of a man who loves every individual without attaching to anyone in particular. Nowhere in the narrative is nature described for its sheer aesthetic beauty. *Pepper* gives a profound vision of man in harmony with his natural world and a close echo of Nambisan's approach to nature is found in Thoreau's *Walden*. Furthermore, Subbu's relationship with the land seems to carry overtones from Wordsworth's pantheism as reflected in the "Tintern Abbey." As a child, Subbu's contact with nature was physical and sensuous: "There were so many thirsts to quench and wasting time in classrooms seemed so pointless. Learning, Subbu reasoned could wait till old age when the only thing worthwhile in one's body was the mind. Life now was meant for dizzy pleasures" (*Pepper* 40). As a youth he craved for the presence of nature and dreams of Kodagu– "the stickiness of bubbling earth, the smell of rotting leaves that fell from the sprawling jackfruit and athi trees, and the itching from the sweat that cooled his back" (*Pepper* 137). Later on in life a subdued power of experience overcomes him and endows him a sublime and blessed mood which lightens the burden of the world:

Nambisan advocates the healing power of nature in her text. Nanji prescribes innumerable remedies to the locals for various illnesses but when she sees her husband in throes of mental depression, she suggests he go for hunting. She feels the hardships of the jungle would help him uplift his spirits. Thoreau suggests in *Walden* that hunting is one of the best parts of man's education which brings him in "closest acquaintance with nature" (141). Nature guides her in the form of her ancestors and educates her. It could also be possible to consider the grandmother of Nanji who constantly guides her in life, to be Mother Nature herself. For Nanji nature had been her classroom. She wishes for Subbu to be educated and simultaneously "wonders if education had anything to do with the practicalities of living" (139) as the children of the soil like the Yeravas, the Kudubas were able to bring up their children without any of it. Thus, through her portrayal of Nature in the novel, a purely regional entity is metamorphosed into a cosmic experience.

Besides dwelling on the bounties of nature, the text also voices a plea for preserving the ecology of the region. Nambisan has expressed her concern over the disappearance of tigers in Kodagu. The issue of deforestation too finds a mention in the novel. Subbu mourns the loss: "People talked of loving trees but cut them down without regret, as if the money they got in exchange would replace the loss" (*Pepper* 262). In the narrative, one finds nature at times partaking human qualities. Subbu dreams of the trees standing at his window encircling his throat with their "newly sprung leafy arms": "You let us be killed, you let us be killed... see how it feels. The branches scratched him and he woke weeping" (263). Here, Nambisan is making use of the trope of pathetic fallacy to impart a sense of the unbroken sympathy between man and nature. The novel carries Thoreau's message that a man's first step in redeeming himself is to let nature be (*Walden* 137).

The novel debates the issue of the Other of Kodagu, the original inhabitants who have been neglected for ages, both by the local and national elites. In the pattedars meeting held at Rao Bahadur's house, the issue of the marginalised groups of Kodagu is taken up for discussion: "But how many Yeravas, how many Kudiyas or Kurubas own even a patch of land? How many of their children go to school, how many can read a newspaper or get a job other than that of a labourer? We are exploiting them, without even realizing that we do it"(66). The Diwan exhorts the Kodavas to stop living in their glorified past and uplift these 'other' of Kodagu–the Yeravas, Kurubas, Kudiyas and Amma Kodavas. Their upliftment lies not in the mere acts of charity but in striving to make them realise their potential for work. Nanji passes on her zest for work to the indolent Yeravas and shows them that "it was more fun to work than to be lazy" (*Pepper* 9).

Indigenous cures and practises resist their integration into the health system propounded by this sort of reasoning. Many such cures have been valorised in *Pepper*. Nambisan, having been educated in England on the Western concepts of medicine would have experienced this in her encounters with the locals during her rural practices. A notable feature of *Pepper* is that one finds medicine constantly being pitted against a home remedy or an indigenous cure. When the pregnant Nanji was down with malaria, she had been prescribed quinine. On realising that the baby did not kick as usual, she took gooseberry wine and "a lehyam of jiggery, asafoetida, almonds and til smothered in ghee to counter the effect that the quinine might have had on the baby" (27). Nanji cured her son's lameness by applying tiger milk ointment prepared by a Kuruba woman on his legs. Such mysterious cures are beyond the empirical rationality of science. Other ailments like burns and wheezing also have their local remedies. Nanji values pepper for its magical properties. She has a handful of pepper tied to the edge of her sari from the day of the dramatic birth of her son, Subbu till the very end – thus imparting the novel its intrinsic title. Nanji accidentally realises that the vet's medicines for animals worked quite well for humans. Baliyanna being the vet acknowledges this and attends to his human patients accordingly. These cures highlight the fact that the cure lies in the faith and the faith has to be generated in the self. The main emphasis of the text thus becomes a repudiation of the western concepts of modernity which enforce a kind of cultural imperialism upon the local and indigenous cultures.

After India achieved independence, Kodagu like the other regions enters into a phase of modernisation. The Kodavas get loans, buy tractors and other irrigational equipments which increases their yield of paddy and coffee. Co-operatives fix fair prices, the Coffee Board is established and the Kodavas become a rich race. As Nambisan admits: "Even in the days when they had lived on wild meat, bamboo, crabs and mushrooms and could barely scratch together enough money for a bus journey to Bangalore, they had the air of wealth about them. Now it became a reality" (244).

Nambisan validates this concept of Indian modernity through her text. The close bonding they share with the land endows them a rootedness which is not found in other regions. For Murphy "a civilised harmony still exists between the landscape and the people" (102). Even when they move out in search of jobs, they have one or more branches of their clans living in the ancestral home to look after the land. In *Pepper* while Subbu's brothers leave home, Subbu stays back with his mother helping her with the work on their land. The fact remains that the call of the land is so irresistible that it finally draws them back to its fold. Towards the end of *Pepper*, Subbu perseveres to emphasise this fact regarding his land and race. He realises that the truth of their destiny lies in their roots:

For all their stylish ways, the Kodavas now were no different from their ancestors. The sophistication was a shell. You were what you were, the children of Thadiyandamolu, Malethirike and Brahmagiri. You had that kernel of honour and fearlessness and were born to care for the land made sacred by the goddess and protector of Kodagu. (245)

For Nambisan, the rustic Concord, an economically backward town free from the evils of industrialism evident in other areas of Massachusetts resembles her land of Kodagu. Like Thoreau, she wishes for her people a region where men would not be dwarfed by external persuasions but would devote themselves to the pursuit of self-culture. The bonding of her characters with the ecology of the land leads to the realisation of the self which allows her characters to remain firmly rooted to the land, eventually liberating them.

Works Cited

1. Emerson, Ralph Waldo. *Essays: First and Second Series.* New Delhi: Eurasia, 1972. Print.
2. Fetterman, David M. *Ethnography: Step-by Step.* California: Sage, 2010. Print.
3. Malinowski, Bronislaw. "The Role of Myth in Life." *Sacred Narrative: Readings in the*
4. *Theory of Myth.* Ed. Alan Dundes. Berkley: U of California P, 1984. 193-206. Print.
5. Nambisan, Kavery. *The Scent of Pepper.* Rev. ed. New Delhi: Penguin, 1996. Print.
6. Interview by Mishra, Deepa. Writing with the Scalpel. 24 May 2011.
7. www.museindia.com. Web. June 2011.
8. "Re: Hello." Message to Nisha Nambiar. 7 Oct. 2011. E-mail
9. Prabhakaran, N. *Kodagu Kurippukal.* Kannur: Kairali, 2008. Print

10. Srinivas, M.S. *Religion and Society among the Coorgs of South India.* New Delhi: OUP, 2003. Rpt. 1952.
11. Thomas, Owen. *Henry David Thoreau: Walden and Civil Disobedience.* New Delhi: Prentice Hall, 1986. Print.

Battling With the Ecological Ego: Mahasweta Devi's *Bitter Soil* As Docufiction

- Dr. Rajshree Trivedi

Bio: **Dr. Rajshree Trivedi** is Principal and Head, Department of English at Maniben Nanavati Women's College- Re-accredited with ' A' by NAAC and affiliated to SNDT Women's University, Vallabh bhai Road, Vile Parle West, Mumbai 400056.

Abstract:

In this chapter, the principles of ecopsychology, a branch of psychology has been applied to the reading of Mahasweta Devi's short stories anthologized in *Bitter Soil*. Certain theoretical terms such as "ecological ego," "ecological unconscious," "environmental reciprocity" and "ecofeminist" ideology will be studied in this chapter with a special slant and emphasis on spatial, social and situational conditions of the personae in Devi's works.

Keywords: ecology, ego, degradation, collusive madness, therapy

An offshoot of psychology, ecopsychology, as a theoretical term, was first introduced in 1992 by Theodore Roszak in his book *The Voice of the Earth*. Basically, the ecopsychologists examine the establishment and connections between human mind and nature and strongly advocate the retreat to nature as therapy for psychological imbalances. Alyson Pompeo-Fargnoli, an ecofeminist, attributes the emergence of ecofeminism as a strong reaction to "a toxic mindset of domination and control that degrades both women and the environment" (2018:1) which is also a major concern of study for ecospychologists. Roszak's theory of ecopsychology suggests a few therapeutic solutions to work on this degradation. He borrows the psychological term "ecological unconscious" and enunciates that the "repression of the ecological unconscious is the deepest root of collusive madness in industrial society; open access to the ecological unconscious is the path to sanity" (Roszak, 1992: 6). More than industrialization and urbanization, the major (and long prevailing, too) effect, on the human psyche and non-human entities in the last two centuries has been caused by colonization and wars. The direct consequence of it has been dislocation and alienation. While the field of psychology has concentrated on devising therapies to heal the alienation between person and person, person and family, person and society, ecopsychology "seeks to heal the more fundamental alienation between the person and the natural environment" (6).

Mahaweta Devi's works have repeatedly been described as "docufiction." As an activist, she closely interacted with the Adivasis of Purulia, Munda, Palamau, Jehanabad, Kuruda, Hesadi, Jarkhani and other areas that fall in the states of Bihar and West Bengal. The indigenous tribes labelled as "criminals" by the British government during the precolonial as well as post-independence times have been reduced to the state of landlessness, poverty, unemployment and cultural distortion. The tragedy of India at independence, she believed [was] not introducing thorough land reform. A basically feudal land system was allowed to stay. A feudal system is anti-women, anti-poor people, against toiling people. It is the landowners who formed the ministry, and became the rulers of the country. why should they do anything else? ('Telling History,' 2002, xv)

In the same interview to one of her critic-translators, Devi raises an outcry against "criminalization of politics, letting the lumpen loose in the lower caste and tribal belts. Inhuman torture and oppression. [and] resistance. [and the] continuing struggle" (2002: ix). Spivak further establishes a theoretical consideration where Devi's prose continuously attempts to [bend] into full fledged "historical fiction, history imagined into fiction. The division between fact (historical event) and fiction (literary event) is operative in all these moves. Indeed, her repeated claim to legitimacy is that she researches thoroughly everything she represents in fiction" (*In Other Worlds,* 2006: 336).

In the light of reading Devi's selected texts from the point of view of Subaltern studies, Spivak suggests, "fiction of this sort relies for its effect on its "effect of the real" (336). Historical narratives such as Devi's short fiction are "a bit of both in. both cases." Like her protagonist Jashoda in 'The Breast-Giver,' Spivak metaphorizes India as a 'mother -by-hire." Interrogating the deeply prevailing infectious patriarchal mindset and the cultural sham of worshipping the Mother figure, Spivak advocates Devi's protest:

All classes of people, the post-war rich, the ideologues, the indigenous bureaucracy, the diasporic, the people who are sworn to protect the new state, abuse and exploit her. If nothing is done to sustain her, nothing given back to her, and if scientific help comes too late, she will die of a consuming cancer. I suppose if one extended this parable, the end of the story might come to "mean" something like this: the ideological construct "India" is too deeply informed by the goddess-infested reverse sexism of the Hindu majority. As long as there is this hegemonic cultural self- representation of India as a goddess-mother (dissimulating the possibility that this mother is a slave), she will collapse under the burden of the immense expectations that such a self-representation permits. (337)

Spivak observations are obvious outbursts to the flawed socio-cultural trait of mother-worship system but at the same time they sound to be narrow interpretations of what requires a more secular outlook in terms of saving the nation(s) from what environmentalists call "planetary crisis" or "ecological crisis." A more serious attention and action by multiple agencies on the planet are expected to operate on a colossal as well as collective level.

The giver is always to be revered, irrespective of any beliefs or ideologies that social or religious theorists fundamentally draw upon for institutionalizing norms or customs. Survival and existence when challenged need to be addressed from more solemnly universal and engaging multiple perspectives. Colonization, industrialization, urbanization and more recently the onslaught of digitalization have witnessed the horrors arising as a result of ecological unconsciousness that has wrapped the minds of the human kind. From anthropocentric to biocentric is the current paradigm shift to break the myth of supremacy of the human race. Environmentalists advocate "biological egalitarianism—recognition of the intrinsic worth of everything in nature—in order to restore ecological harmony of the world" (Alyson: 2)

Although Mahasweta Devi's docufiction seems to raise an alarm against the so-called developmental policies of governmental and capitalist agencies by exploiting the marginalized, they, in fact, represent the "voice of the earth." They cross the peripheral vicinities of tribes, clans, communities and societies to speak for all those who are at the receiving end. If her texts speak for the "lumpenproletariat," they also speak for the "bitter soil," "seeds," "salt," "hillocks," "ravines," "forests," and "coal mines under the earth." They speak for the burning earth and air on the mythological battlefield of Kurkshetra that had been turned into a cremation ground with heaps and heaps of rotting dead bodies waiting to be cremated ('the five women' in *After Kururkshetra,* 2005: 10-11) after the great war was over. The short story certainly speaks volumes of the catastrophic and devastating scenes left by the two historical World Wars followed by many cold as well as clandestine ones that the nations fight in a more contemporary situation.

"So the sole purpose of my writing is to expose the many faces of the exploiting agencies," surmises Mahasweta Devi in 'Introduction' to *Bitter Soil And Other Stories* (1998: ix). Further, she enlists, "the feudal-minded landowner, his henchmen, the so-called religious head of the administrative system, all of whom, as a combined force" who join hands to exploit and contribute to the "lop-sided development" of India have to be exposed. In her more direct statement, she declares:

I have not written these stories to please my readers, if they get under the skin of these stories and feel as the writer feels, that will be reward enough. [These] stories written in 1980s are becoming whatever is written in these stories What she states is the reflection of hideous contemporary realities everyday in India. Whatever is written in these stories is continuing unabated. So where is the time for sleep? The situation demands immediate response and action. (1998: x)

Mahasweta Devi, in fact, raises the fundamental question, "Are we ecologically unconscious?" (Roszak, 2).The "combined force" is operative out and ought to be driven to self-realization. Samik Bandyopadhyay, another critic-translator of Mahasweta Devi's works notes:

It is an illegitimacy that Mahasweta Devi locates throughout society, in the administration, in the cultural-intellectual establishment, in politics, in the existence of the whole antisocial fringe of killers prepared to serve the interests of any organized political force anywhere between the extremes of the Right and those of the Left. In a narrative style that allows simultaneously for an evocation of the illegitimacy rampant at all these levels as more than a setting and focussing on an individual's independent self-realization ('Introduction,' *Mother of 1084*. 2001: viii)

Glenn Albrecht, a philosopher and professor of sustainability at Murdoch University, Perth coined a term- "solastalgia," a combination of the Latin word *solacium* (comfort) and the Greek root *–algia* (pain), which he defined as "the pain experienced when there is recognition that the place where one resides and that one loves is under immediate assault ... a form of homesickness one gets when one is still at 'home'(quoted by Smith, 2010, np).The other important terms that Albrecht uses are 'place pathology" and "psychoterratic syndromes" that diagnoses mental-health issues attributable to the degraded state of one's physical surroundings.

Mahaweta Devi's short stories (four in all) in *Bitter Soil* problematizes the basic ecopsychological issues such as mental anxieties, hallucinations, grief, unsettledness, restlessness, despair resulting out of displacement, conflict or natural disaster-affected zones in the backdrops of poverty, illiteracy and unemployment mingled with caste based hierarchical status of the people residing in the villages of Toru, Juhujhar, Lohri, Hesadi and Kuruda located in between the territories of Bihar and West Bengal. The plight of these inhabitants is by no means local. Mining of iron, sand and coal in quarries, open-pit mining, polluting of rivers and streams, oil spills in oceans and on lands, deforestation, increasing wastelands and other man made disasters are serious concerns related to environmental risks.Albrecht calls it a "global condition"- the ongoing degradation of the environment. "Little Ones' documents the social, moral, cultural and biological degradation of the Aagariyas, the aboriginal iron and coal miners of Kubha (a hilly forest settlement) in the Lohri village. Mahasweta Devi describes the "damned terrible place" as:

[the] entire area is a burnt-out desert. As if the earth bears a fire of unbearable heat in her womb. So the trees are stunted, the breast of the river, a dried out cremation ground, the villagers dim behind a film of dust. The earth is a strange colour. Even in the land of red earth, such a deep brownish-red is rarely seen. Of course, before fresh blood dries and congeals, it just turns such a dark, lifeless red. (1)

The Aagariyas were believed to belong to the *asura* clan and it was only their community that was allowed to enter "the netherworld and bring back iron. Only the Aagariya." (*Bitter Soil,*4). During the immediate post-independence times:

[the] Bharat *sarkar* sent people to search for iron ore in Lohri. The villagers of Kubha were troublemaking Aagariyas. They said- Our three demon gods live in that hillock. Don't dig that up. Two Punjabi officers, a Madrasi geologist, why would they believe in these *junglee* tales of *asur deotas*? They blasted the hillock flat. (5)

The outcome was "The Aagariyas of Kubha attacked and cut down everyone. Then they vanished into the jungle (5). The far-reaching effect of this forced dislocation was starvation and alienation. In a surrealist manner, the story ends on a note of shocking discovery made by the newly appointed relief officer in the famine-stricken Lohri village that the actual stealers of the relief material were none other but the Aagariyas who were reduced to the size of pygmies due to continuous starvation. Thus, revolt for saving their own land had transformed them into "ghoulish vengeful" adult-children.

In Roszak's theory:

This great act of collective alienation, I have suggested, lies at the root of both the environmental crisis and individual neurosis. In some way, at some point, a change of direction, a therapeutic turning inward, had to take place within a culture as maniacally driven as ours has been by the need to achieve and conquer. (2002:276)

For the Aagariyas, there is no "therapeutic turning inward" but a persistent state of "individual neurosis" for all the fourteen members left out of the 154 fugitives. On the other hand, for the relief officer, the terror they cast upon him by the pygmied Aagariyas, circling naked around him, is an experience where empathy overshoots fear or anger against them. It becomes a pathway to experience a catharsis that leads to "liberation:

Standing under the moon, looking at them, hearing their laughter, feeling their penises on bis skin, the undernourished body and laughable height of the ordinary Indian male appear a heinous crime of civilization. He feels like a criminal condemned to death... [They] dance, they laugh, scaly penises brushing against him, his only liberation lies in going mad, rending the atmosphere with the howl of a demented dog. But why isn't his brain sending the order for this throat shattering stream? Tears stream from his eyes. (20)

The deliberate reference to the agents of change for the betterment of the planet is made in the story with reference to World Health Organization, Christian missionaries, government appointed Block Development Officers, relief centres and the religious bodies.

The rich calorie food when not consumed for the normal development of a human body is "construed as a crime by the World Health Organization." This is what the relief officer believes. For the Aagariyas, the only way to survival is to resort to the act of crime of stealing. Against it, for the relief officer. "If this is true, then all else is false. The universe according to Copernicus, science, this century, this freedom, plan after plan." (19) The sum of everyone's happiness if, is the sum of all happiness, the synergy seems to have been broken. And this is the fundamental tenet of Roszak's theory. He deduces:

Ecopsychology holds that there is a synergistic interplay between planetary and personal well-being. The term 'synergy' is chosen deliberately for its traditional theological connotation, namely that the human and divine are cooperatively linked in the quest for salvation. Or in contemporary ecological terms: the needs of the planet are the needs of the person, the rights of the person are the rights of the planet. (Roszak, 1992:7)

Dulan Ganju, the 'lowborn old man in the short story 'Seeds,' finds solace and redemption from all his sins in sharing the harvested paddy with his fellow villagers. Dulan had been gifted this piece of land by Lachman Singh, the "powerful Rajput *mahajan* of Tamadih. The place is described as:

[uneven], arid, sunbaked. The grass doesn't grow here even after the rains. The occasional raised serpent hoods of cactus plants, a few neem trees. In the middle of this scorched wasteland where no cattle graze is a low-lying boat shaped piece of land. Around half a *bigha*.(21)

Dulan's apparent day time preoccupation of life was to guard crops on this land that comprised of "aloe plants, leaves thorny like the pineapple" but beneath this façade of being the " Lord of a thorny wasteland," he had been guarding the land that buried the dead bodies of Lachman Singh's victims. subtle, dark overtones mixed with dry, black humour, Mahasweta Devi unfolds the agonizing story of Dulan and taps the moral, philosophical, spiritual thresholds between the person and his or her 'ecological ego.' It finds maturity much on the planes of social relations or cultural obligations rather than being operative on political or lawful forces. In eco psychological terms, "The ecological ego matures toward a sense of ethical responsibility to the planet that is as vividly experienced as our ethical responsibility to other people. (Roszak,1992: 8) The "fundamental alienation between the person and the natural environment" can be restored only by giving and sharing, by love and empathy, by giving it back to nature. Dulan's efforts exactly exemplify the "ethical responsibility" he has towards the land he had polluted and the need to depollute it. The answer lies in turning all the dead bodies of Lachman's victims to "seeds." Having shared all his paddy harvest, Dulan returns to his land. His heart is strangely wonderfully light today! [Karan]. Asrafi, Mohar, Bulaki, Madhuban, Paras and Dhatua-what an amazing joy there. Is in the ripe green paddy nourished on your flesh and bones!Because you will be seed. To be a seed is to stay alive. Slowly, Dulan climbs up the *machan*. A tune in his heart. Stubbornly disobedient. Returning time and again. Dhatua made up this song.. Dhatua-Dulan's voice trembles as he says the name. Dhatua, I've turned you all into seed. (56)

Among the victims, Dhatua was Dulan's son who had rebelled against Lachman Singh's exploitative policies against the labour. Dulan's silence over his own son's burial in his "wasteland" becomes instrumental in relieving the villagers from Lachman Singh's malpractices.

Whether it is the privileged or unprivileged, victim or victimizer, *mahajan* or *pahaan,* the suffering and redemption of Mahasweta Devi's people are closely woven with the earth and her therapeutic measures. The earth is not a "rightless realm" but an entity that the human, inhuman, sub-human and non-human must integrate this idea in their ecological consciousness. Both, *Ekoa*, the mad elephant in the jungle of Palamou and Purti Munda, "the most vocal personality" from the adivasi village of Jhujhar in the story "Salt" violate the norms of nature. Mutual co-existence and harmony are what the planet has offered unconditionally to all the species on the earth and the penalty for invading each other's terrain or exploitation of resources is death which is the end of all agonies.

Salt, the most essential "inorganic and mineral constituent of the body"(131) is the cheapest available commodity in the consumers' market for humans and the same is true of the animal kingdom for whom the mineral is easily available ingredient of soil. Apart from the mainline story which seems to be a stretched, exaggerated imagination of Mahasweta Devi's oeuvre of historical fiction, the plot insinuates the fundamental right of existence denied by power and tyrannical forces. Behind the story lies the colonial struggle led by Mahatma Gandhi for Indian independence and freedom from the British rule. The famous Dandi March and the salt *satyagraha* against the heavy taxes laid by the British government on the Indians. It was an act of nonviolent civil disobedience movement that continued for 24 days against the salt monopoly of the British rulers.

Uttamchand, the village *mahajan*'s monopoly in Jhujhar for selling salt and then withdrawing its sale from all his shops is reminiscent of the atrocious crimes committed by the British Raj. Such an act was a reactionary response to the *satyagraha* launched by the villagers against the *betbegari* (wageless labour). On comparing the events-Dandi March and Jhujhar's non-violent ways of handling the salt crisis- one realizes that the common enemy was the political force that disallowed the basic rights of people. In Jhujhar's case, the animal kingdom is also affected because of the human actions. After the struggle with Uttamchand, the conflicting party changed from him to *ekoa* whose saltlicks Purti and friends started invading. A similar situation was witnessed in the post-independence era when the British left but the new enemies were the existing feudal lords joining hands with the newly formed government's ministers who were more opportunists than the former ones. In both instances, there is a "collusive madness" that hosts the repression of "ecological unconsciousness" (Roszak, 1992:1) of not being sensitive to the needs of the millions who are deprived because they have no access to avail their rights on the planet. Roszak's advice, thus is:

Whatever contributes to small scale social forms and personal empowerment nourishes the ecological ego. Whatever strives for large-scale domination and the suppression of personhood undermines the ecological ego. Ecopsychology therefore deeply questions the essential sanity of urban-industrial culture, whether capitalistic or socialistic in its organization. It counsels that we "scale down, slow down, decentralize, democratize. (1992:8)

It will not be a hyperbolized statement that India, like Jhujhar, was driven to "saltless darkness" in the post-independence era. Mahasweta Devi's concern was an extension of all her Marxist ideological constructs. Her voice against the establishment has been documented in her fiction making it more of the "leftist intellectualism and struggle" (Spivak, 1981:385)

Maysar Sarieddine, an ecopsycholgist at the Lebanese-American University, Lebanon argues in her paper 'Oppression and Violence Against Women: An Ecopsychological Perspective' (2018):

The issue of violence against women has been discussed, debated, lobbied, and fought for in recent decades; and much research on the incidence, reporting, and implications of such violence against women has also been conducted in many regions and countries. These concerted activist efforts led to the first declaration that recognized the need to provide women the rights to equality, security, liberty, integrity, and dignity of all human beings. Even with such global efforts, and despite the existence of laws that punish men who perpetrate violence against women, the problem continues to persist worldwide (2018:np)

Ecopsychology examines the "parallel split between nature and humanity and between women and men" (Sarieddine, 5). Barring 'Little Ones' and 'The Witch,' the other two stories in *Bitter Soil* do not project female personae who are directly shown to be the victims of the patriarchal order. Nonetheless, all the four stories do strongly have an undercurrent of the exploitation of resources lying in the womb of Mother Earth. The female figure in 'The Witch' paradoxically is shown in a reverse form- a different one than the otherwise archetypal image of *stree* as a form of *shakti*.In the Indian context furthermore, she is a birth-giver, nurturer, creator, producer and in many other socially accepted stereotypical forms. *Daini* who is equally a symbol of power and strength is associated with famine, chaos, terror, death, blood, nakedness, calamity and anything that disturbs the normal life style of villagers of Tura. She is the one who can shake the foundations of the patriarchal order. The only weapon to combat her is collectively stone her to death.

Mahasweta Devi's witches are actually the victimized and not the victimizers. In yet another story 'Bayen,' Chandi Dasi, like Somri in 'The Witch' are the victims of jealousy and lust, respectively, who have been forced to turn into *dainis*. In both figures, the reflection of earth as a female, ruthlessly corrupted, polluted and exploited for vested interests, throws back the mirror image of a society contaminated by inequality, injustice and indifference that would lead humankind to the brink of destruction. Such an approach unquestionably asks for a revaluation of "compulsively masculine character traits' and offer remedial measures to curb them.

Mahasweta Devi's fictive texts are woven with the threads of historical facts and well blended with folklore, songs, narratives, legends, mythological renderings and popular material of the region she selects as locales for her narratives. With the use of surrealist techniques, humour, sarcasm and docu-linguistic-corpuses, Devi is able to draw a large number of registers so as to add richness of language on one side and ferocity of words on its other side. By doing so, she intends to push her reader to develop a strong sense of social and moral responsibility so as "to awaken the inherent sense of environmental reciprocity that lies within the ecological unconscious."

References:

Mahasweta Devi (2005). *After Kurukshetra* (translated by Anjum Katyal). Seagull: Calcutta.

___ (1995) *Imaginary Maps*. Trans. by Gayatri Chakravorty Spivak. London. Routledge.

----- (1997) *Breast Stories*. Trans.by Gayatri Chakravorty Spivak. Calcutta Seagull Books.

----- (1998) *Bitter Soil*. Trans. by Ipsita Chandra. Calcutta: Seagull Books.

-----(2001) *Mother of 1084*. Trans. by Samik Bandyopadhyay.Calcutta: Seagull Books.

-----(1994) *The Book of Hunter*. Trans. by Sagaree & Mandira Sengupta. Calcutta: Seagull Books

-----(2002) *Chotti Munda and his Arrow*. Trans. by Gayatri Chakravorty Spivak.Calcutta: Seagull Books.

----- (2004) *In the Name of the Mother*. Tran. by Radha Chakravarty. Calcutta: Seagull Books.

Pompeo-Fargnoli, Alyson (2018). 'Ecofeminist Therapy: From Theory to Practice' in *Journal of International Women's Studies*, Volume 19 | Issue 6, Aug-2018, pp. 1-16

Roszak, Theordore (1992). 'The Voice Of The Earth: Discovering The Ecological Ego' in *Trumpeter*, pp. 1-6

(2002) *The Voice of the Earth: An Exploration of Ecopsychology*. Phanes Book, USA,

Sarieddine, Maysar (2018) 'Oppression and Violence Against Women: An Ecopsychological Perspective.' *Clinical & Experimental Psychology*. Vol.4 (1), 189, pp.1-8.

Spivak, Gayatri Chakravorty (2006). *In Other Worlds:Essays in Cultural Politics*. Routledge, London,pp. 271-370.

(1981). '*Draupadi* by Mahasveta Devi.' *Critical Inquiry*. Vol.8, No.2, Writing and Sexual Difference (Winter 1981), pp. 381-402.

Weblink:

Smith, Daniel B. (2010) 'Is There an Ecological Unconscious?' in *The New York Times Magazine*. Jan. 27, 2010.https://www.nytimes.com/2010/01/31/magazine/31ecopsych-t.html#story-continues-1

Contemporary Women Nurturing Family in Urban Dwelling: *Yoshimoto*

- Dr. S. Sridevi

Bio: **Dr. S. Sridevi** is an Associate Professor in the Research Department of English at Chevalier T. Thomas Elizabeth College for Women, Chennai-11.

Abstract:

This paper aims at studying the novella *Kitchen* as a metaphysical journey into sustenance and energy creation. The existing criticisms for Yoshimoto's works read her works as a result of emergence of *shojo manga* in the 1980s such as 'ladies comics,' and globalization. Though Mikage Sakurai, the young woman narrator of the story, is a product of Japanese urbanization, and the novella is seen as a work of popular culture or paraliterature, the fact that Yoshimoto's work has become a transcultural bestseller reaching out to contemporary readers creates a need to investigate how she projects the domestic space. Is she projecting the sphere of a home as a superior being of metaphysical nature with the capacity to heal? Also, gender construction and contestation and fluid identities are presented in Eriko, the father/mother of Sakurai's friend Yuichi Tanabe, who becomes a woman to take up the powerful role of a mother. On the superficial level, the story seems to celebrate cooking, and at a deeper level it challenges the conventions of society and uplifts the role of women and attempts to fashion human dwelling and reiterate it as a space for security, comfort and metaphysical bliss without the traditional authority systems. When Ambai puts down the cultural and political position of the kitchen,

Yoshimoto appears to celebrate kitchen like a domesticated woman, but presents transgender issues, liberal women and Americanized lifestyles with a smooth poise.

Keywords: domestic space, dwelling, Yoshimoto

Banana Yoshimoto's writing has been critiqued for being superficial, capitalist text. This paper argues that Yoshimoto's writing can be read as an example of a paraliterature that is significant because of its exploration of themes of metaphysical nature, usually associated with literariness, using a popular culture style. The domestic space has a politics of survival and offers its members spiritual sustenance is a major theme operated by Yoshimoto. A home offers a metaphysical locale for the soul to recuperate and reenergize itself, and this space is under the control of women that perhaps male philosophers could not call it theirs and therefore Heideggerian homecoming and Levinas' hospitality themes are located outside homes. Homes, for men represent something secretive which they consider as limiting their scope and from this dogmatic western philosophical position a home naturally becomes a socially inferior location.

> Heidegger suggests that homelessness, or exodus, is a fundamental and necessary element of homecoming. Writing of Holderlin's hymn to the Danube, Heidegger describes the river as a place of home and journey. In its essence, the river is the —locale of human dwelling; ... Just so, - coming to be at home in one's own itself entails that human beings are initially and for a long time, and sometimes forever, not at home. (Eubanks 27)

In "Introduction to Metaphysics," Heidegger makes use of philology to construct the ambiguity in the concept of a home. The German word *unheimlich* is the opposite of *heimlich*, which means "familiar" and "native." It also shares a semantic kinship with heimisch, that which belongs to the home. *Heimlich* can also mean "secret" or "concealed" (Leichter 155).

> While human being is secure in its home, such security comes with a price: specifically, security allows human being to hide its own being from itself. The uncanny thus exposes human beings in two senses: it displaces them from their familiar modes of understanding, valuing, and thinking, and it discloses the tendency to hide and find security from one's very being. (Leichter 157)

Heidegger argues that "modern politics exacerbates the plight of homelessness that ails the modern West." In Levinas's terms "the self is compelled to welcome the Other into the public space of the homeland and the private space of the home" (Eubanks10-18).

The private space of the home and the communal space of homeland integrate in the domestic space where Yoshimoto does not contest the existing philosophical location of the kitchen. Instead, she delves into understanding the role it plays in maintaining the sanity of people and emphasizes its role in human development. Using a Levinasian angle of thought Sakurai becomes 'the other' who is welcomed into the home of Yuichi as a welcome gesture offering solace, but Sakurai takes up a higher role in their friendship guiding him.

Yoshimoto's writing has brought in two types of criticism: one reads her works as a product of Americanization; the other reads them as postmodern texts moving away from the boundaries of 'high' and 'low' art. Her works present a world portraying a "transitional society polarized by changing ideals of femininity." A few critics call

Yoshimoto's writing as a "separatist literature of inner space." Yoshimoto is widely read in Japan and abroad and "can be seen as a trans-cultural writer. Her success is thus helping to redefine contemporary literature both within Japan and overseas" (Martin 8). Internationalization and egalitarianism became goals for Japan in the 1980s. "Trans-border flows of capital, goods, technology and people" reached "new heights." Cultural diversity, global discourses of gender and multiculturalism became the hallmark of the 1980s (McCormack 2).

Banana Yoshimoto's original name is Yoshimoto Mahoko, and she was born in 1964, Tokyo, Japan. Her father, Takaaki (Ryūmei), was an intellectual, critic, and a leader in the radical student movement in the late 1960s. Yoshimoto's graduation story, *Moonlight Shadow* (1986), earned her the Izumi Kyoka Prize. She gave herself a gender-neutral androgynous pen name - Banana (Kuiper).

Yoshimoto wrote Kitchin, Kanashii Yokan (Sad Foreboding) and Utakata/Sankuchuari (Bubble/Sanctuary) in 1988. Kitchin was translated into Chinese in 1989. Her first English translation, which contained both Moonlight Shadow and Kitchin, was published as Kitchen in 1993. Two Japanese directors, Ishikawa Jun (Tsugumi, 1990) and Morita Yoshimitsu (Kitchin, 1990), adapted her novels to the large screen, and in 1997 Hong Kong director Ho Yim made a Cantonese-language version of Kitchin. Yoshimoto continued to write novels like NP (1990 N.P.), Amurita (1994 Amrita), and Hādoboirudo / Hādorakku (1999 Hardboiled & Hard Luck). Yoshimoto also published short stories, including Shirakawa Yofune (1989 Asleep) and Tokage (1993 Lizard), and essays, including Painatsupurin (1989 Pinenuts [or Pineapple] Pudding), Yume ni Tsuite (1994 About a Dream), and Painappuru Heddo (1995 Pineapple Head) (Kuiper).

The period in which Yoshimoto wrote most of her works is an era of Americanization of values, beliefs, and customs, and the economic boom of Japan reflecting globalised trends, pop culture and a confidence in the people. The novella *Kitchen* captures this positive mood of the Japanese, creating energies of the spirit, drawing sustenance from themselves, from their materials and accepting loss and grief with dignity. Mikage Sakurai has no parents, and has lost her only grandmother; Yuichi has no mother and his father who became a woman also is killed. Yet the novella does not portray angst or existential questions of life reflecting human agony and failure. Instead, the text marches on confidently with not clinging to the past in a negative manner, enjoying the home space, simple things of homes, streets, the sky, light and ordinary people. It celebrates life reflecting the mood of the Japanese presenting their ability to work hard, their perseverance and the tremendous will power the people showed after the Second World War. The novella differs from European postwar writings in its presentation of life. It takes the route of metaphysics as a source of strength and nourishment to revive the human spirit.

The Allied Occupation (1945-1952) "dismantled the Japanese empire, abolished the armed forces," and brought changes in education, the constitution, civil code, family, and economy. The purpose was "to demilitarize Japan and foster democratic institutions, ideologies, and attitudes." The "Japanese will, know-how, and energy along with American procurements during the Korean War brought about economic recovery by 1955 and a position as the number two economy in the world by the late 1970s." This period shows high dynamism in society as Japan became an advanced economy. Japanese consumer products had such high quality that there was a demand for them all over the world (Molony 6). From the 1980s, ideas deriving from linguistic and critical theories have influenced Japanese historiography and Japanese gender studies. Themes of gender construction and contestation have characterized research on gender in Japan (Molony 7).

Gender construction is discussed by Yoshimoto in an easy conversation between Mikage Sakurai and Yuichi. Yoshimoto does not present the complexities of transience, the psychological difficulties and the conflict in the son's mind in accepting the change in the physical makeover of the father into a mother. This scene throws challenges to tradition and swiftly breezes in changes in gender perception and it is located in the domestic space, changing its rooted role-plays and presents the Japanese society as a trans-friendly culture. The post-operative issues of transgenders and their trauma are not described as a reader might expect at this point of the story which suddenly leaps forward informing us that Eriko who gets into a mode of commodified femininity, was actually a man earlier.

In the early 1980s, two new Japanese-English neologisms appeared: *'newhalf'* and *'Mr.Lady'* which designated entertainers who had ... undergone varying degrees of surgical reconstruction. Creation of the term *newhalf* dates back to 1981 and is attributed to Betty, the Mama of the Osaka show pub *Betty's Mayonnaise*... Betty's catchphrase ... was 'I'm half man and woman' (otoko to onna no hafu). 'Half' or 'hafu' in Japanese language is a term commonly used to refer to individuals of mixed race, usually Japanese and Caucasian. Betty, who styled herself as a 'new half,' was therefore another indeterminate figure, not of mixed race but of mixed gender. This term ... was picked up by the media... Suptsu Nippon ran an article about Betty entitled 'Gay singer named Betty is called a newhalf'. However, it was the massive media attention given to 'Roppongi girl' Matsubara Rumiko in May of that year that ensured the new term became widespread. Matsubara, while hiding her biological status as a man, had won a beauty promotion staged by businesses in Roppongi (a popular Tokyo nightlife area), becoming the cover girl for a poster campaign promoting the area's clubs and bars. Once her transgender history was revealed, she was quickly elevated to idol status (McLelland 10).

The Japanese audience obviously did not expect Yoshimoto to get into a detailed description of the trauma of shifting from a male identity to a female. Eriko, legitimated as a woman, speaks in a "slightly husky" voice. Her hair "rustles like silk to her shoulders." Her "long, narrow eyes" have a "deep sparkle." Her "lips" are "well formed." The nose has a "high, straight bridge." She vibrates with a "marvelous light" and "life force." She looks like a goddess and Sakurai remembers that "she didn't look human." Eriko rushes out and runs to the door in her high heels, her "red dress flying" (Yoshimoto 11). Sakurai is reminded of the warm light emitted by Eriko softly glowing in her heart and is dazed. Yuichi, after dropping Eriko at the night club realizes that Sakurai is overwhelmed:

"Mikage," he said, "were you a little bit intimidated by my mother?"

"Yes," I told him frankly. "I've never seen a woman that beautiful."

"Yes. But..." Smiling, he sat down on the floor right in front of me. "She's had plastic surgery."

"Oh?" I said, feigning nonchalance. "I wondered why she didn't look anything like you."

"And that's not all. Guess what else – she's a man." He could barely contain his amusement.

This was too much. I just stared at him in wide-eyed silence. I expected any second he would say, "just kidding." Those tapered fingers, those mannerisms, the way she carried herself... I held my breath remembering that beautiful face; he, on the other hand, was enjoying this.

"Yes, but..." My mouth hung open. "You've been saying all along, 'my mother' this, and 'my mother' that..."

"Yes, but. Could *you* call someone who looked like that 'Dad?' he asked calmly. He has a point, I thought. An extremely good answer.

"What about the name Eriko?"

"It's actually Yuji." (Yoshimoto 12-13).

In Japan, "Individuals have constructed" their "fluid identities," resulting in "ambiguity" which has "characterized notions of gender identity as well as gender norms. Variability in gender performance, including performance of sexuality in the early modern period" which "reinforces the salience of ambiguity in constructions of gender" says Molony (8). The 1980s was a time of Americanization of Japanese society with "champagne, garish colors and bubbly disco dance-floor anthems." The economic boom back then helped draw Japan's women into the workforce (Saito). The period came to be known as the golden age of idols and a pool of celebrities were indigenized through television programmes. Generally referred to as an era of bubble economy, Japan became a "post-industrialized society organized around information and consumption" (Galbraith). The end of the 1980s was marked by a general interest in Japan because of the country's ongoing economic boom (Havranek 125).

Yoshimoto has naturally absorbed and inherited the Japanese Seitō (Blue Stockings) movement which has become a legacy. Hiratsuka Raichō (1886–1971), the founder of Seitō; Takamure Itsue (1894–1964), the first feminist women's historian and poet; and anarchists such as

Kanno Sugako (1881–1911) were revolutionary women who defied gender norms (Shigematsu 6) who have laid a path for twentieth century women writers to liberate themselves from Japanese traditional systems of thinking and writing.

The Italian version of *Kitchen* became a bestseller and won the Scanno Literary Prize in 1993. Nevertheless she is referred to as "the perfect pop-culture disposable author" because she is a typical writer who is completely indifferent to literary tradition and uses a very simple writing style derived from comic books, animation, films, popular songs, and TV (Haga 12). American readers constructed and renewed images of contemporary Japanese women by reading the novels of Banana Yoshimoto as a representation of Japanese shojo-culture at the end of the 1980s. ""Shojo" literally means "girl" in Japanese, and "shojo-culture" is pop-culture mainly consumed by young, Japanese women" and "John Whittier points out that shojo culture is a symbol of contemporary Japanese consumer capitalism, and Yoshimoto's works are one of the typical representations of shojo-culture" (Haga 71).

Patricia Smith—in order to find out why Yoshimoto's *Kitchen* was so popular in Japan, selling more than a million copies—used stereotypical terms or phrases such as "polite in the Japanese manner," "Japanese literary sensibilities," and "the author's delicate strokes," which were often used by American critics to describe Japanese literature and culture. Other reviewers also mentioned characteristics of traditional Japanese literature and culture in the novel. For example, Scott Shibuya Brown used a classical Japanese phrase "mono no aware," which means pathos or sensitiveness to beauty feeling the mutability of everything in the world and missing something lost, to explain why this novel had such a great popularity in Japan. Deborah Garrison said that she saw the spirit of Zen in the heroine's spiritual feeling in a scene in the story ... Elizabeth

Hanson said that the heroine of the novel was a typical representation of young Japanese women, who were attracted to kitchens and cooking as signs of comfort and womanliness and tried to live independently. (Haga 74)

When *Kitchen* was first published in Japan, many Japanese critics, especially older males, paid attention to her unique writing style that had been largely influenced by contemporary Japanese comics and light novels for young women, and many of the critics praised the novel as something new in Japanese literature. "Yoshimoto's writing isn't itself very complex; it skips lightly over the surface of even Mikage's darkest hours" (Haga 75).

> It also helps to bear in mind that Japanese is a language expressed in brush-stroke kanji images rather than alphabetical and grammatical abstracts... And although every language has its inherent beauty, kanji images evoke an entirely different sensation for the reader than do mere words on the printed page. Therefore, the sensual experience of reading in kanji, not to mention elements such as alliteration, onomatopoeia and honorific language, are often lost in translation. (Heiter)

Yoshimoto's writing that attempts to heal and its search for spiritual meaning and a reconnection with nature has an added significance at a time when urbanisation is accompanied by the breakdown of community and family structures. "Criticism of Yoshimoto's writing suggests" that it is "either the product of late capitalism, or else that it reflects the changing nature of Japanese society by showing young women making alternative life-style choices" (Ramsay 13).

The novella *Kitchen* opens dramatically with a resounding and arresting statement: "The place I like best in this world is the kitchen. No matter where it is, no matter what kind, if it's a kitchen, if it's a place where they make food." The kitchen that is described by Yoshimoto has "lots of tea towels" and is "dry and immaculate" with "white tile catching the light (ting! Ting!)" Yoshimoto 3). She presents a mythic world in Jungian sense, acquiring an inner comprehension of peace and solace. Working in the kitchen becomes a ritual act for Mikage Sakurai who narrates the novella that "raises the human individual to the dignity of a metaphysical factor" to quote a phrase from Jung (253). The domestic space lifts the human mind:

> This curious behavior of my dreams corresponds, incidentally, to a phenomenon which was noted during the First World War. Soldiers in the field dreamt far less of the war than of their homes. Military psychiatrists considered it a basic principle that a man should be pulled out of the front lines when he started dreaming too much of war scenes, for that meant he no longer possessed any psychic defenses against the impressions from outside. (Jung 273)

The home is then the 'psychic defense' for a man confronted with life and death issues like a war. For a woman, inside the home, there is yet another special place which becomes her psychic defense – a metaphysical comfort zone. Yoshimoto is said to create a pathos of transience (*Vergänglichkeitspathos*) in her works. The motif of transience is described as part of Japanese tradition, related to the realm of fantasy (Havranek 135-8).

Mikage Sakurai is comforted by the hum of a refrigerator as after she loses her only relative in the world, she is still in a daze, unable to sleep. She moves to her "gleaming kitchen" the fridge gives her company. "The long night came on in perfect peace, and morning came," and she starts sleeping "in the kitchen day and night" (Yoshimoto 5).

The external world has dangers and home is a "safe fold and the warm cocoon" giving "protection from inner stress." People on "the road to individuation" will soon find themselves "with the positive and negative aspects of human nature." As "the psyche" possesses its "inner polarity," which is a prerequisite "for its aliveness," and "an ego was possible" with the need for "opposites" to "achieve a state of balance." Jung further describes this energy born out of the opposites:

> The energy underlying conscious psychic life is preexistent to it and therefore at first unconscious. As it approaches consciousness it first appears projected in figures like mana, gods, demons, etc. whose numen seems to be a vital source of energy, and in point of fact is so as long as these supernatural figures are accepted. But as these fade and lose their force, the ego that is, the empirical man seems to come into possession of this source of energy, and does so in the fullest meaning of this ambiguous statement (Jung 346).

Can the domestic space be perceived as an archetypal memory of the cave man to signify safety and security? The men in the novella, Yuichi Tanabe and Eriko bring Mikage Sakurai to create a home environment to heal all three of themselves. Yuichi's house has all the elements for a spiritual rejuvenation and healing for Sakurai – "a kitchen, some plants, someone sleeping in the next room, perfect quiet." Gratefully she narrates: "this was the best. This place was ...the best" (Yoshimoto 16).

The particular nature of perception portrayed reflects a conditioned consciousness structured as instinctual dynamics. The kitchen creates a spiritual energy in Sakurai giving her strength of will to endure and acquire some kind of godliness – in Jungian sense the superordinate principle. Yoshimoto constructs a spiritual scene playing with a description of light, sky and the kitchen that underplays the shock of accepting Yuichi's father who has become a woman - Eriko:

> The entire apartment was filled with light, like a sun-room. I looked out at the sweet, endless blue of the sky; it was glorious. In the joy of being in a kitchen I liked so well, my head cleared, and suddenly I remembered she was a man. I turned to look at her. Déjà vu overwhelmed me like a flash of flood. (Yoshimoto 17)

Jungian idea of the unconscious wanting to do both the acts of dividing and uniting, the autonomous intelligent unconsciousness of the being unites the shock of itself adjusting with such speed. The soul acts faster creating solace and calmness in accepting the gender change. Deftly, Yoshimoto moves ahead of the story, not pausing to analyse the impact of Eriko's actions and the next paragraph reads as: "The house smelled of wood. I felt an immense nostalgia, in that downpour of morning light, watching her pull a cushion onto the floor in that dusty living room and curl up to watch TV" (Yoshimoto 17).

Already in one of his earliest lectures, entitled "Some Thoughts on Psychology," which he delivered in 1897 while a medical student at Basel University, Jung maintains that the "soul" "extends far beyond our consciousness," and further suggests that this unconscious dimension of the soul is an "intelligence" which is irreducible to conscious intelligence. (Capobianco 50)

Scholars in housing studies describe the domestic space as something connected to a person's mental and physical well-being and is related to many circumstances, not the least of which is the quality of their dwelling and home environment. An important part of such quality is physical design and layout, and how far it enables the ease of people's mobility and movement around the dwelling and the use of different rooms and their facilities (Imrie 745).

It has been well established in housing studies that the home is one of the fundamental places that gives shape and meaning to people's everyday lives ...A burgeoning literature has, in various ways, explored the social, health and psychological effects of the home .... For example, Sixsmith & Sixsmith (1991) note that the home is a symbol of oneself or a powerful extension of the psyche. It is a context for social and mental wellbeing or, as Lewin (2001) suggests, a place to engender social psychological and cultural security. For others, the home is the focus for personal control and a place that permits people to fashion in their own image (Saunders, 1990). In this sense, the domestic setting is, for Lewin (2001), a mirror of personal views and values. (Imrie 746)

Homely actions are realistic and vital they acquire symbolic meanings and do become universal sacraments. Ancient symbols have their origins in the commonplace events (Langer 130). Culture begins at home and the significance of a home expands:

> The basic character of dwelling is safeguarding. Mortals dwell in the way they safeguard the fourfold in its essential unfolding...In saving the earth, in receiving the sky, in awaiting the divinities, in initiating mortals, dwelling propriates as the fourfold preservation of the fourfold. (Heidegger 352-3)

For Jung, a home became the prime symbol of the past, becoming a sacred ground making one feel safe – an extended psychic body, a manifestation of the soul. Hence the rituals of the home also gain significance. Some male thinkers do find the home as a solace like McLuhan and Yoshimoto reinforces this thinking, as homelessness can lead to anarchy.

For Gilman (2002) ... the home was a potential source of repression. In particular, she referred to women's exclusive confinement to the home as leading to 'mental myopia' in which the individual was made into 'less of a person.' Likewise, a range of feminist writers have sought to deconstruct ideal images of the home by suggesting that the home, for some women, is a place of captivity and isolation (Allan, 1985; McDowell, 1983). It is, as Goldsack (1999) notes, "less of a castle, and more of a cage." Others note that the home is as much about the focus for the drudgery of domestic work. (Imrie 747)

Ambai's story "A Kitchen in the Corner of the House" was written in 1988, a year after Banana Yoshimoto's novella, *Kitchen*. Ambai's story illustrates how the patriarchal centre seeks to silence and marginalize the female. Home is seen as a repository of culture, a space of the narrowness and secrecy, as seen by Heidegger. Ambai sees the limitations of home to an individual and rejects the concept of universal cultural identity. Women are refused the freedom to move around freely and thus are losing the opportunity to wander or be free. The spirit is oppressed as even the skyline can't be seen from the kitchen that is described. There is no light at the physical and spiritual level, and one realizes the significance of the word 'corner' in which the kitchen, dark in all aspects is situated.

Right at the end, the kitchen, struck on in a careless manner. Two windows. Underneath one, the tap and basin. The latter was too small to place even a single plate in it. Underneath that, the drainage area, without any ledge. As soon as the taps above were opened, the feet standing beneath would begin to tingle. Within ten minutes there would be a small flood underfoot. Soles and heels would start cracking from that constant wetness...there were green mountains outside the window that looked eastward from the kitchen.... The cooking area was beneath this very window. The green mountains might have made one forget one's chapped heels. But since the clothesline was directly beyond this window, trousers, shirts, pajamas, saris, and petticoats spread out to obscure the view. (Ambai 230-1)

Ambai's kitchen is the very symbol of female oppression where her metaphysical needs are put down indifferently. The domestic space becomes a restricted sphere where her creativity is strangled. The main character of the story Minakshi is disgusted with the food war that takes place in the kitchen. She realizes that "the kitchen was not a place; it was essentially a set of beliefs" (Ambai 233). Minakshi asks her father-in-law to extend the verandah outside the kitchen. She tells him to remove the clothesline that hides the mountains from being seen. Promptly, more clotheslines are added as if to put her in her place. Female hostility is mirrored through the kitchen and food wars in Ambai's long story. Ambai's original name is C.S. Lakshmi, and the pseudonym has tremendous significance as it refers to a powerful woman who takes revenge on Bhishma in *Mahabharata*, by being born again as a man Shikandi. Her writings have a dynamism and power contesting traditional roles allotted to women by patriarchy.

Heidegger's concept of a home refers to rooted communities and differentiates between building and dwelling citing examples of railway stations that do not become dwellings. People do feel comfortable and at home in their places of work, but still these buildings do not connect with their souls. He takes the German word for building – *buan* which means to dwell. The neighbor is the *Nachgebauer*, the near-dweller. "When we speak of dwelling we usually think of an activity that man performs alongside many other activities...The way in which you are and I am, the manner in which we humans *are* on the earth, is *buan*, dwelling." Dwellings are created out of buildings and they tend "the growth that ripens into fruit of its own accord" (Heidegger 349).

In Tamil *veedu* is the word used for dwelling. The word also means salvation. Ambai's story in Tamil reads as "Veettin Moolaiyil Oru Samayal Arai." The story does not use the meaning of salvation, as it refers only to the house as a building in which the kitchen is pushed to the corner. If we use Heidegger's theory of language that argues that "it is language that tells us about the essence of a thing, provided that we respect language's own essence... *language* remains the master of man... language is the highest and everywhere the first," (Heidegger 348) we can analyse why Ambai finds fault with the architecture of a house.

Tamil has another word to refer to a dwelling – *aham*. This word also has another meaning – mind. Tamil literature is divided into two parts – *aham* and *puram*. The word *puram* refers to external elements. *Aham* literature relates to emotions and *puram* literature to external activities. Domestic space is defined by Tamil language as a space for emotions and salvation, if we put all the meanings together.

Cultures differ and Rybczynski says that in the 17th century "feminization of the home" was of primary importance in Holland's domestic interior. "In the Dutch home the kitchen was the most important room" and it was treated with dignity – "something between a temple and a museum." The cupboards held "linens, china, and silver. Copper and brass utensils, brightly polished, hung on the walls. The chimney piece was enormous and elaborately decorated... the sink was copper, sometimes marble." Some kitchens even boasted "interior hand pumps" and "supply of hot water." In Paris, the middle call homes had kitchens that had no direct access to the main rooms. In England, the kitchen was located in the basement until the 19th century (Rybczynski 72-73).

According to our human experience and history, as least as far as I see it, I know that everything essential and everything great originated from the fact that man had a home and was rooted in a tradition. (Martin Heidegger in the interview "Only a God Can Save Us" qtd. By Eubanks 1)

Society's foundation is the domestic space and by celebrating it, Yoshimoto re-establishes the power of women in the family system, as they are in charge of bringing peace unto its members. Sakurai gets a job as an assistant to a cooking teacher and enacts her identity an independent woman. When she sees women who attend the classes, she re-understands life from another angle:

> Those women lived their lives happily. They had been taught, probably by caring parents, not to exceed the boundaries of their happiness regardless of what they were doing. But therefore they could never know real joy. Which is better? Who can say? Everyone lives the way she knows best. What I mean by "their happiness" is living a life untouched as much as possible by the knowledge that we are really, all of us, alone. That's not a bad thing. Dressed in their aprons, their smiling faces like flowers, learning to cook, absorbed in their little troubles and perplexities, they fall in love and marry. I think that's great. I wouldn't mind that kind of life. Me, when I am exhausted by it all, when my skin

breaks out, on those lonely evenings when I call my friends again and again and nobody's home, then I despise my own life- my birth, my upbringing, everything. I feel only regret for the whole thing. (Yoshimoto 59)

These attitudes of popular culture, reinforcing established systems of thought, pave the way for the likeability of the book and probably explain the popularity across the world. At the same time Yoshimoto's Sakurai openly talks about old boyfriends and frankly tells the readers how she loved his hearty robustness, and how now her tastes have changed, and she prefers strange cheerfulness of the Tanabe family and their tranquility. Two contradictory concepts of tradition and modernity that balance each other: presenting the paradox of the human mind and presenting an honest picture of a society at the crossroads of culture and an emerging global economy bringing in trans-cultural negotiations.

After delving into a nostalgic mood for the bygone way of life, Sakurai springs out of this momentary frame of mind and thinks:

> But-that one summer of bliss. In that kitchen.
>
> I was not afraid of burns or scars; I didn't suffer from sleepless nights. Every day I thrilled with pleasure at the challenges tomorrow would bring. Memorizing the recipe, I would make carrot cakes that included a bit of my soul. At the supermarket I would stare at a bright red tomato, loving it for dear life. Having known such joy, there was no going back.
>
> No matter what, I want to continue living with the awareness that I will die. Without that, I am not alive. That is what makes the life I have now possible.

Inching one's way along a steep cliff in the dark: on reaching the highway, one breathes a sigh of relief. Just when one can't take any more, one sees the moonlight. Beauty that seems to infuse itself into the heart: I know about that. (Yoshimoto 59-60)

Carrot cakes and supermarkets and even the highway of Yoshimoto's descriptions are what a young educated woman of 1980s in the fast developing and westernized Japan would think of and if we ignore this realistic portrayal, we see the moonlight. We meet the young Sakurai who thinks: "in this world there is no place for sadness. No place; not one" (Yoshimoto 23). It is here the novella acquires the metaphysical status described by critics as esoteric. To Sakurai the "blackness of the cosmos" is "total science fiction" (Yoshimoto 4). Sakurai is moving to her friend Yuichi house with her luggage, moving out of her old apartment she had lived with her grandmother until she died. She is dead tired and lonely:

My angry, irritable reaction to the jarring each time the bus lurched to a stop told me how tired I was. Again and again, with each angry stop, I would look outside and watch a dirigible across the far-off sky. Propelled by the wind, it slowly moved along.

Staring at it intently, I felt happy. The dirigible traversed the sky like a pale moonbeam, its tiny lights blinking on and off.

Then and old lady sitting beside her little granddaughter, who was directly in front of me, said in a low voice, "Look, Yuki, a dirigible. Look! Look! Isn't it beautiful?" (Yoshimoto 33)

The dirigible moves Sakurai and the grandmother reminds her of her own grandmother and the tough Sakurai's heart melts, softens and tears pour down her cheeks wetting her blouse and she herself is surprised by her tears. The tears are flooding out. She gets down from the bus and sobs for the first time. The moonbeam heals her and washes away her sorrow and purifies her soul in a cathartic manner. She implores to gods: "Please, let me live" (Yoshimoto 35).

Healing and drawing sustenance looks like Yoshimoto's main engagement and even Eriko is given a dialogue to express her views on becoming independent to face the challenges of life. As she is watering the plants in front of the terrace Eriko tells Sakurai that "it is not easy being a woman." There are "many, many difficult times." To enable strength of mind, "if a person wants to stand on her own two feet" it is important to undertake "the care and feeding of something. It could be children, or it could be house plants." These responsibilities help us "understand" our "own limitations." Sakurai tells us: "As if chanting a liturgy, she related to me her philosophy of life" (Yoshimoto 41).

The reference to Momoko Kikuchi (the translator Megan Backus calls her Momoko Sakuchi) with a popular romantic song also refers to moonlight and sunshine. Kikuchi's addition in the novella is fixed in a dream sequence for Sakurai – a popular touch, a local chord, the pulse of the readers. Yoshimoto does not pretend to write only for the highbrow, and consciously puts elements into her text to connect with the public – as an entertainer – the primary purpose of art.

Nature – the sky, air, plants and especially light, emerges as a strong spiritual symbol giving sustenance to Sakurai against black gloom, sometimes emanating from people and sometimes from nature, in *Kitchen*: "window stars" (4), "I just wanted to sleep under the stars" (5), "I wanted to wake up in the morning light" (5), "He seemed to glow with white light" (Yuichi) (7), "the whole of her gave a marvelous light" (Eriko) (11), "There was a warm light.. softly glowing in my heart" (12), "Their faces shone like buddhas when they smiled" (15), "the atmosphere, sparkling, replete with moisture, refracted the glittering night" (16), "the entire apartment was filled with light, like a sun room. I looked out at the sweet, endless blue of the sky; it was glorious" (17), "little by little, light and air came into my heart" (21), "a warm, golden sunlight filled the empty rooms I had once called home" (32), "the winter moon ... was almost full and shed an incredible brightness" (61), Eriko has been the dazzling sun that lit the place (87), I felt strangely light hearted. I was excited. Alone under the stars, in a strange place (89) etc. The connection with natural elements and seeking a spiritual calmness, a kind of Asian spirituality with an American lifestyle brings in a hybridized contemporary transcultural being, who is still located in the domestic space celebrating its components of food and shelter symbolizes the novella *Kitchen*.

Sakurai is amused that her proximity to nature extends even in her choice of men: "For some reason I keep getting connected to men who have something to do with plants" (Yoshimoto 23). Yuichi has plants in his flat. Sotaro, her old boyfriend loved parks, green places, and open spaces and in school he used to sit among greenery.

There are too many deaths in this story – Sakurai's parents, and grandmother; Yuichi's parents (one of them is murdered) – and out of this existential gloom and darkness, Yoshimoto attempts to construct a story of optimism and hope using the Japanese style of writing with *kanji* images, invoking pictures of nature and trying to live close to the universe – all in the strict and defined domestic space. Now and then the angst thrashes directly especially when Sakurai tells us after the death of Eriko, a victim of hegemonic masculinity of a fan at the nightclub: "A door opened before us that night – the door to the grave" (Yoshimoto 54). Grappling with multiple deaths is a major task of Sakurai and Yuichi and with limited number of characters; the novella negotiates with human frustrations in a limited geographical sphere with a rich scatter of nature's images. The young Sakurai analyses her loneliness and sad plight after the death of the only relative she had: To the extent that I had come to understand that despair does not necessarily result in annihilation, that one can go on in spite of it, I had become hardened. Was that what it means to be an adult, to live with ugly ambiguities? I didn't like it, but it made it easier to go on." (Yoshimoto 56)

> Mortals dwell in that they initiate their own essential being – their being capable of death as death-into the use and practice of this capacity, so that there may be a good death. To initiate mortals into the essence of death in no way means to make death, as the empty nothing, the goal... Dwelling itself is always staying with things. Dwelling, as preserving, keeps the fourfold in that with which mortals stay: in things...mortals nurse and nurture the things that grow... (Heidegger 353)

Heideggerian approach to dwelling makes it a space for preserving and womanhood from this position appears to be in charge of preservation. And this dwelling is controlled by women who design the patterns of its operations. Sakurai and Eriko are the women created by Yoshimoto, not as victims of society confined to the domestic sphere, but as preservers and nurturers of the spiritual self and sanity of the members of the domestic space which is fluid and accepts new members with a postmodern ease. The margins of the dwelling are not defined in a fundamental and inflexible manner as one would expect in a supposed to be conservative Japanese society. Yoshimoto re-carves a space for women like Sakurai, who rip open structures, hardly conscious of their unconventional modes of operation in the narrow space of family. The concept of family is expanded including people who are not related to each other through blood, defining a new system of kinship pattern.

Is Sakurai a preserver of dwelling, a maintainer of relationships and a nurturer of life? The novella has a cathartic effect on the general reader, as it has carefully selected components of small doses of elements of healing that communicate with clarity. After the murder of Eriko, after mourning for days, at last in an effort to face death and accept the reality, Sakurai and Yuichi heal themselves by cooking an elaborate meal and eating it well. Nightmares and daydreams haunt their minds and they move in and out of depression, nevertheless fighting with all their spirits to grapple with life. "Living things were connected to the sun," (Yoshimoto 81) says Eriko explaining why she has a terrace garden, as when she was a man, his sick wife, before her death, wanted some living things inside the house.

Chika is upset about Eriko's death and Sakurai philosophizes: "It was true that she (Chika) jumped to conclusions and that her life was a mess... but the beauty of her tears was something I would not soon forget. She made me realize that the human heart is very precious." (Yoshimoto 86)

Also the novella proves another point: "The kitchen, a symbol of female oppression in another age as the domain of the housewife chained to the kitchen sink, is thus reclaimed by Yoshimoto as a place for creativity and self-expression, rather than enforced domesticity." (Ramsay 102)

Is Sakurai also a modern girl, a product of Japanese feminism, Americanization and with fluid notions of self-identity? Eriko has written a letter to her son Yuichi which is read after her death: "Please tell her (Sakurai) hi. And tell her to stop bleaching on her legs in front of boys. It is indecent" (Yoshimoto 53). The middle class educated women like Sakurai are modern with western ideas of beauty and style, constructing new ways of being carrying new ideals of femininity in an evolving society shaking out of the disasters of the world wars.

The term "Modern Girl" ... first appeared in 1923... She was one of the thousands of female factory workers, employees in newly emerging professions, retail workers in both modern department stores and tiny retail shops, bus conductors and telephone operators, café waitresses, highly trained employees in teaching, medicine, and other sectors, and privileged young women who could easily afford international products and fashions. As a media sensation, the Modern Girl was transgressive. Common criticisms focused on her supposed foreignness, frivolousness, and promiscuity. Both Marxist and conservative critics called Modern Girls "hedonistic" and "decadent." Most, however, were hardworking employees with working-class or middle-class jobs. (Molony (2018) 5)

The hybridized and trans-cultural reality of the 1980s Japan and its new middle class and the new woman are carefully presented by Yoshimoto using a very attractive writing style invoking nature and probably poetic in its original Japanese. The fact that even in translation this quality of literariness is coming through perhaps will explain the way the book has endured rigorous criticism from European countries and America and still manages to be read all over the world. Its positive and enriching way of approaching the domestic space is re-writing the feministic portrayal of domestic space, culinary skills, man's fundamental need – cuisine and its production, the spiritual role played by victuals and womanhood itself. The urban educated woman is constructed as an individual who is in charge of the dwelling, who creates a sanctuary for man and serves her purpose of life and acts as the foundation of culture and civilization re-viewing the patriarchal notions of "women's place" and "women's work" as positions of sustenance and superior. The novella can also be seen as a feminist strategy for domestic reform, not by critiquing existing social systems, but by presenting a globalised model of home in which the educated woman of strong will and intelligence commands and takes care its members inventing a new kind of housekeeping, and probably this aspect makes it a utopian fiction or paraliterature or popular culture to traditional systems.

Works Cited

1. Ambai. "A Kitchen in the Corner of the House." *A Purple Sea*. Short Stories. Translated from Tamil by Lakshmi Holmstrom. Madras: East West Books, 1992.

2. Capobianco, Richard. "Heidegger and Jung: Dwelling Near the Source." Review of Existential Psychology and Psychiatry, 21:1-3 (1993), 50-59. Web, June 14, 2019.

3. Eubanks, Cecil L., "David J. Gauthier. The Politics of the Homeless Spirit: Heidegger and Levinas on Dwelling and Hospitality." https://pdfs.semanticscholar.org. Web, June 14, 2019.

4. Galbraith P. W., J. G. Karlin. Idols and Celebrity in Japanese Media Culture. Springer, 2012. Web. 20 April 2019.

5. Haga. Tadahiko "Translating Contemporary Japanese Culture: Novels and Animation." PhD.Thesis, Stony Brook University. 2012. Web. 27 May 2019.

6. Havranek, Erich. "Corroded by Globalisation: The Image of Japanese Literature in German Review Articles." Vienna Journal of East Asian Studies, Volume 6, eds. Rudiger Frank, Ina Hein, Lukas Pokorny and

Agnes Schick-Chen. Vienna: Prae-sens Verlag, 2014. Web. 27 May 2019.

7. Heidegger, Martin. "Building, Dwelling, Thinking." Translated from German by Albert Hofstadter. Basic Writings. Ed. David Farrell Krell. Harper Perennial, 2008.

8. Heiter, Celeste. "Book Review: Kitchen by Banana Yoshimoto." Things Asian. Jan 6 2002. Web. 15 April 2019.

9. Imrie, Rob. "Disability, Embodiment and the Meaning of the Home" [2004] Housing Studies. 19:5, 745-763. Web. 15 April 2019.

10. Jung, Carl Gustav. Memories, Dreams, Reflections. Translated from German by Richard and Clara Wilson. Vintage Books. 1989.

11. Kuiper, Kathleen. "Banana Yoshimoto. Japanese Writer." *Encyclopedia Britannica*. Web. 15 April 2019.

12. Langer, Susanne K. A Study in the Symbolism of Reason, Rite, and Art. Philosophy in a New Key. A Mentor Book, The New American Library. Sixth Printing, June 1954.

13. Leichter, David. The Poetics of Remembrance: Communal Memory and Identity in Heidegger and Ricoeur. e-Publications@Marquette. Marquette University, 2009. Web, June 14, 2019.

14. Malony, Barbara. "Feminism in Japan - Oxford Research Encyclopedia of Asian History." Department of History, Santa Clara University, 2018. (oxfordre.com/asianhistory) Web, June 17, 2019.

15. McCormack, Gavan. "Introduction." Multicultural Japan: Palaeolithic to Postmodern. Ed. edited by Donald Denoon, Mark Hudson, Gavan McCormack. Cambridge University Press, 2001.

16. McLelland, Mark J. "From the Stage to the Clinic: Changing Transgender Identities in Post-war Japan." Research Online. University of Wollongong, 2004. Web, June 14, 2019.

17. Molony, B., & Uno, K. "Introduction." In B. Molony & K. Uno (Eds.), Gendering Modern Japanese History (pp. 1–35). Harvard University Asia Center, Harvard University Press, 2005.

18. Ramsay, Martin. "Single Frame Heroics: New Ways Of Being In The Fiction Of Yoshimoto Banana." Ph. D Thesis. Swinburne University of Technology, 2009. Web. 27 May 2019.

19. Rybczynski, Witold. Home: A Short History of an Idea. Penguin, 1986.

20. Saito, Mari. "Bright Lights, Big Shoulder Pads: A Timid Japan Recalls Its Bubble Era." The New York Times. April 6, 2018. Web. 29 April 2019.

21. Shigematsu, Setsu. Scream from the Shadows: The Women's Liberation Movement In Japan. University of Minnesota Press, 2012.

22. Yoshimoto, Banana. Kitchen. UK: Faber & Faber, 1994.

Reading between the lines: the construction of Carter's postmodern women in *The Passion of New Eve*

- Shweta D. Salian

Bio: Shweta D. Salian, an Assistant Professor in English at Mithibai College of Arts, Science and Commerce, Vile Parle, Mumbai, specializes in Postmodernism, Postcolonialism, Marginal Literature, Subaltern Literature, Indian English Literature and Diaspora.

She is M.A., N.E.T. in English Literature. She has done her M.Phil from the University of Mumbai.

Recently, she has submitted her Ph.D. thesis to the University on: *Gender, Picaresque and Magic Realism: A Postmodern Interpretation of Angela Carter's novels.*

She has presented several research papers in prestigious colleges of Mumbai and has been invited to deliver guest lectures.

Abstract:
The representation of women in works of literature has been multitudinous over the years. Ranging from dealing with the condition of women in general, to a minuscule observation of the story of a particular woman, fiction writers have been trying over decades to create awareness in the minds of their reading public. Angela Carter deconstructs feminine ethics laid down by age old stalwarts like Plato and Sade, to create a distinctive ethics of her own. In her fiction, she gives us a variety of postmodern women existing and fictional to show

us the array of possibilities that we otherwise chose to deny in our orbit of existence. In her attempt to lash at masochism, she subverts the existing male dominated fiction to accommodate her women characters in a way that the men are at their mercy. Carter is clearly invoking an air of exoticism, eroticism and fantasy to push realism beyond its limits. By doing this she breaks the limitations set for women in the fiction of her time. Boundless, seamless and timeless, Carter's fiction can be gleefully relished by readers of all ages with a brave heart. This research paper attempts to look at some of the female characters in Carter's fiction, particularly in *The Passion of New Eve*, to understand the manner in which she deconstructs established identities.

Keywords: feminism, postmodern, identity, subversion, deconstruction

Reading between the lines: the construction of Carter's postmodern women in *The Passion of New Eve*

Postmodernism empowers the writer to induce in writing, the solipsistic pleasures of word play. It shows the writer's self-reflexive interest in the processes of narrative itself. The hyper-reality of postmodern fiction allows the text to connect with the reader while maintaining a sense of aloofness that continues to shock the reader through the magnificence of simulacrum. *The Passion of New Eve* deconstructs the grand narrative to give a new meaning to the process of genesis of the woman, while giving due recognition to the developments in medical science that has allowed multifarious possibilities in the evolution of the human body.

The Passion of New Eve by Angela Carter, is a parody of primitive notions of gender, sexual difference and identity from the perspective of postmodern feminism. The sadomasochism in the novel is visible specifically in the portrayal of Leilah and Evelyn by Carter. On the whole, the novel employs the politics of power that keeps shifting from one power centre to another, From Evelyn to Mother and Lilith, to Zero, to Eve who is the savior and Evelyn's transformed self. The transformation of Evelyn to Eve is the locus around which the plot and subplots in the novel revolve, to emphasize the celebration of feminine consciousness in Eve.

Carter ironically equates the unconscious with the feminine and consciousness with the masculine. The representations of the feminine also vary from the romantic or erotic anima figures to the powerful and menacing Mother whom the male ego (the centre of consciousness) has to fight and from whom he should liberate himself. The moment Evelyn sets foot in Beulah, he finds that there is a semblance of fallen masculinity that appeals him:

> It was a pompous structure, chipped out of granite dragged from god knows where, it was twenty or thirty feet tall. It cast an infinitely elongated shadow in the direction of the night; upon a classic pediment, it represented a stone cock with testicles, all complete, in a state of massive tumescence. But the cock was broken off clean in the middle; upon the fractured surface, a vulture with the look of a hanging judge perched and, as I thought, winked at me most horribly. The top half of the cock, ten feet of it, lay in the

sand at my feet but it did not look as if
it had fallen accidentally. (p.44)

Identity and gender is constantly deconstructed in the novel, so much so that it is in a state of flux among the characters. Evelyn is the best example of this phenomenon although it is difficult to ascribe a certain gender or identity to him/her. Tristessa too, falls under the category of false notions furthered by the medium of movies to her spectators like Evelyn who fall in love with the onscreen identity of the actress/actor. Only when Eve meets her in person towards the end of the novel, does she realize that Tristessa offers possibilities of love and fantasy to the genderless viewer; both men and women can enjoy her companionship.

In the beginning of the novel, Evelyn discloses his fantasy lady, his goddess who taught him to love. His subservience is visible in the beginning itself:

> Tristessa. Enigma. Illusion. Woman? Ah! And all you signified was false! Your existence was only notional; you were a piece of pure mystification, Tristessa. Nevertheless, as beautiful as only things that don't exist can be, most haunting of paradoxes, that recipe for perennial dissatisfaction. (p.2)

Tristessa is the silent movie star actress is a she-male. Her silence is a compulsive need of patriarchy to be allowed to dominate her moves. Her identity is kept a secret from the audience so as to increase her popularity among the youth, "For you were just as beautiful as you had been twenty years before, would always be so beautiful as long as celluloid remained in complicity with the phenomenon of persistence of vision..." (p.1) Thus the screen is responsible for Tristessa's created/onscreen image that will freeze her age forever in the eyes of her audience.

Evelyn is obsessed with Tristessa since youth dawned upon him. He used to jerk off her at movies by gawking at her feminine form on the 'silver screen', "I took some girl or other to the movies and, through her mediation, I paid you a little tribute of spermatozoa, Tristessa". (p.1) At that point in time, Tristessa appeared to him as a female goddess who was unattainable. Nevertheless, his intense emotions for Tristessa ends up in his encounter with her at her glass house, the premonition of which he receives in the event of his changing cities and jobs:

> I abandoned myself to nostalgia, to the ironic appreciation of the revisited excesses of her beauty. I thought I was bidding a last goodbye to the iconography of adolescence; tomorrow, I would fly to a new place, another country, and never imagined I might find her there, waiting for revivification, for the kiss of a lover who would rouse her from her perpetual reverie, she, fleshy synthesis of the dream, both dreamed and dreamer. I never imagined, never. (p.5)

The change in the identity of Tristessa causes discontent to Evelyn, who had idolized her. Like any average boy in his teens, he discounts her appearance by adorning his walls with her presence:

Tristessa had long since joined Billie Holliday and Judy Garland in the queenly pantheon of women who expose their scars with pride... Her stills became posters; she inspired a style for one season, they named a discotheque after her, and a chain of boutiques. But I myself had loved Tristessa out of pure innocence when I was a little boy and the sculptural flare of her nostrils haunted my pubescent dreams. The wall of my cubicle at school had been plated with her photographs. (p.3)

Tristessa does not stop at being a movie star. Yet it is difficult for Evelyn to accept Tristessa as any other girl next door as she appears in the poster. For him she is the goddess, whom he ogles at, who is beyond his reach; anything but the girl next door. He writes to MGM about his discontent at their change in her appeal but all he "received, in return for my (his) ink-stained, illspelt love-letter, (was) a still from The Fall of the House of Usher, she, ethereal in her shroud, just risen from her coffin to the manner born." (p.3.)

Evelyn lusts after Tristessa, finding her divine; but this heightened illusion that Evelyn harbours is mocked by MGM when they add insult to injury by transforming Tristessa into a flat-chested woman. Carter subverts the symbolic image of the bulging bosom that is a point for ogling for men. Carter also subverts the theory of castration of Lacan, where Evelyn, a man, is seen wanting something that he lacks; that is a pair of breasts and a vagina. Thus, Carter brings out quite the obvious in human nature; the man woman relationship originates from lacks and fills quite different from one another.

She had been the dream itself made flesh though the flesh I knew her in was not flesh itself but only a moving picture of flesh, real but not substantial. I only loved her because she was not of this world and now I was disillusioned with her when I discovered she could stoop to a pretence of humanity. I therefore abandoned her. I took up rugby football and fornication. Puberty stormed me. I grew up. (p.4.)

Leilah, one of Evelyn's girlfriends, is presented as a sexual object, a prostitute for a purpose in the early part of the novel:

She had on a pair of black, patent leather shoes with straps around the ankles, fetishistic heels six inches high and, in all the heat and paranoia of summer, an immense coat of red fox was slung around her shoulders; I will always associate her, with some reason, with foxes. (p.15)

Yet, Leilah learns it the hard way that once the purpose of man is served, the objectified woman ceases to be. Impregnated and scorned by Evelyn in the early part of the novel, Leilah assumes the transformed self of Lilith, a soldier in the clan of the Mother.

In the first few pages of *The Passion of New Eve*, Carter introduces the acquired self of Leilah while she dresses herself up for going to Nightclubs or theatres or restaurants where she performed. The act of dressing is described elaborately by Evelyn who is the sole spectator of the 'dress-up show'. He is the representative of the 'male gaze' while he 'adores' watching Leilah "I would lie on her bed like a pasha, smoking, watching, in her cracked mirror, the transformation of the grubby little bud who slumbered all day in her filth..." She is given the title of the Lily in the mud which is metaphorical of her existence to fulfil the filthy passions of a man like Evelyn.

Destiny serves him right when Evelyn finds himself in the city of Beulah, where he undergoes the process of transformation. A woman soldier, feeds him clothes him and prepares him for the exchange to happen in the near future between him and mother by citing the famous Greek tragedy, the story of Oedipus, who impregnated his mother and killed his father; " She spoke to me once. She said: 'Oedipus was the most fortunate man in the world, for he embraced his fate with pleasure.'"

Initially, Evelyn is overwhelmed by the figure of the mother, the many breasted goddess. She has made herself, every part of her:

> Mother has made symbolism a concrete fact. She is the hand-carved figurehead of her own, self-constructed theology... The great, black, self-anointed, self-appointed prophetess, the self-created god-head that had assumed the flesh of its own prophecy was the destination to which her unknowing acolyte had no option but to lead me; one woman is all women... Leilah had lured me here, at last; Leilah had always intended to bring me here, to the deepest cave, to this focus of all the darkness that had always been waiting for me in a room with just such close, red walls within me. (p. 55)

The tables are turned with Leilah assuming authority over Evelyn's body who is instrumental in shaping his body to look like Eve's with Mother's advanced medical skills.

Evelyn marvels at the goddess like appearance of Mother, who has a beard like Queen Hatshepsut did. The beard symbolizes masculinity; the same beard that was shaved off Evelyn's face, that he will never be able to see again. That which is Mother's has disappeared for all eternity from the face of man, "Her head, with its handsome and austere mask ... as big and as black as Marx' head in Highgate Cemetery; her face had the stern, democratic beauty... she wore a false beard of crisp, black curls like the false beard Queen Hatshepsut of the Two Kingdoms had worn... she possessed two tiers of nipples... of a strenuous programme of grafting, so that, in theory, she could suckle four babies at one time."

Evelyn ends up being a woman Eve which is a play of the 'Circle of life'. Carter makes Mother impregnate Eve with the seed that Evelyn furthered after being propelled by Mother:

> So I was unceremoniously raped; and it was the last time I performed the sexual act as a man, whatever that means, though I took very little pleasure from it... she clasped her muscles together and expelled me just as my seed pumped helplessly out and I rolled over the floor, yelping, leaving a snail track of gasped gobs of semen in my wake. (pp. 61-62)

The entire act of forced impregnation is mankind's act of self-rape; a self-induced domination of the self. Carter smudges the borders of biological domination of the sexes to suggest an empathetic outlook on gender hierarchy. The figure of the mother is a self-created imaginative power that shows the mirror to the sadomasochistic male.

The villainous one-eyed Zero subjects Eve to eternal damnation by his acts of subjugation, forcing himself upon her. By allowing Zero to dominate her, Eve is seeking a kind of a retribution for Evelyn's past acts. The abduction and rape of Evelyn by the Mother and the consequent abduction and rape of Eve by Zero is significant of the theory what goes round comes round, "When he had finished, he rose, zipped up his leather fly and said: 'Congratulations. You've just become the eighth wife of Zero the poet.'" This reduction of Eve to the object that he earlier saw women as, culminates in the circular movement of the novel.

Carter has enabled Tristessa, the Hermaphrodite figure in the novel, to have a deifying act on Zero as the latter claims that she took away his masculinity from him through a spiritual action. Thus, in her fiction, Carter brings in people, induces an interaction between them along with free expression endorsing unacceptable behaviour and promoting it as one's natural expression. She includes bold profanities and bodily acts that otherwise involve privacy, to be openly exhibited all over her prose as if the very aim of her writing is to shock the average conforming morally driven reader.

Her female characters are free of stereotypes and gender defined roles as observed in *The Passion of New Eve*. Rather, the word 'passion' in the title of the novel is synonymous with a punny reference of the passions that are carnal in nature and the passions that are the struggles that her protagonist Evelyn has to undergo in order to become the Biblical Eve. Her transformation is the literal man to woman transformation where Eve is born out of Evelyn. Carter has taken care to induce enough symbolic references to suggest the synonymy between the sexes; endorsing the fact that gender is a construct that is socio-cultural in nature.

Works Cited

1. Carter, Angela. *The Passion of New Eve*. UK, Virago Modern Classics, 1982.
2. Butler Christopher. *Postmodernism: A Very Short Introduction*. Oxford University Press, 2003.
3. Carter, Angela. ''Notes from the Front Line'' in *On Gender and Writing*. 1983.
4. Crofts, Charlotte. *Anagrams of Desire*. New York: Manchester University Press, 2003.
5. Derrida, Jacques. *Writing and Difference*. London: Routledge, 1981.
6. Dutheil Hennard, de la Rochere. *Reading, Translating, Rewriting: Angela Carter's Transnational Poetics*. Detroit: Wayne State University Press, 2013.
7. Eagleton, Terry. *The Illusions of Postmodernism*. London: Wiley-Blackwell, 1996.
8. Gamble, Sarah. *The Fiction of Angela Carter*. ed. New York: Palgrave Macmillan, 2001.

A Transcendental and Eco-critical Reading of Sunil Sharma's political novel *The Minotaur*

- Dr. Sangeeta Sharma

Bio: Dr. Sangeeta Sharma currently heads the department of English, B. K. Birla College of Arts, Science and Commerce (Autonomous) College, Kalyan, Mumbai, Metropolitan Region. She has authored three books and has edited five anthologies on poetry, fiction and criticism, solo and joint. She is a recognized PhD Guide in English Literature by the University of Mumbai.

Abstract:

Sunil Sharma is in the vanguard of the contemporary fiction written in Indian English today. He has an enormous output of short fiction and poetry as well. Basically, a Marxist-text, but multi-layered, scholars are finding his novel highly relevant to assess the power -and wealth-driven modern societies. His debut novel, *The Minotaur,* is a master narrative that depicts the struggling humankind, groping for intellectual answers to old existential problems of the inequity of wealth and power, justice and good governance, and, oppression of the liberals. In short, the enduring human desires for a more humane, better, fair and livable world for everybody. The novel is divided into an epilogue, eight chapters and an afterword. The most astonishing fact is the vision of the writer towards nature and its treatment at his hands. He has found nature to be a source of profound meaning, tranquility and knowledge. Today, when there is a revived interest and lot of discussion over the reclamation of nature from mindless exploitation by man, it can be discerned that the writer in the very first decade of the twentieth century has posited wilderness with serenity, beauty, mysticism and spirituality. Nature has been delineated as life-giving and as a timeless marvel. The current paper deals with the transcendental and eco critical reading of this seminal text. It is an attempt to analyse and trace the writer's oblique but remarkable portrayal of the virtues manifested in nature.

Keywords: Nature, jungle, wilderness, transcendentalism, spiritual

Sunil Sharma in *The Minotaur* gives a chilling but familiar account of the rise and fall of a third-world despot. Riding the tidal wave of popular support, Caesar, the Marxist, soon turns into a dictator and plunges his impoverished, exploited nation into a bloody civil war. Fleeing from his burning nation, he lands up in a remote island and declares himself the king. Then the personal descent of a once charismatic doctor-turned-guerilla leader into personal hell begins. The Minotaur is born and finally finds his nemesis, in the form of a radicalized native, on that remote island.

In the very first chapter, as the scene opens on Caesar, the protagonist who has survived, the second time, his close brush with death after his jet has run into an unexpected storm, lost its altitude and has crashed due to a technical snag or human error, he finds himself on an alien shore looking at the light crimson sky. A beautiful account of Nature meets the eye:

> The morning appeared glorious. The immensity of the blue Pacific was humbling experience for the tiny

survivors, stretched out on the white sands, ordinary mortals shorn of office, dominated bythe thickly wooded hills in the back. The thick impenetrable jungle, deep and mysterious, started almost at the edge of the white sands, so near you could feel its moist breath tingling your naked skin and also clearly hear hissing of leaves and overhead melody of bird songs in interlaced branches of tall trees. The air was languid and atmosphere tranquil, turning into a heavenly setting which their hungry eyes found pretty soothing: the entire place generating a feeling of strange timelessness and primeval solitude, almost suggesting eerily the very beginnings of Time itself in that obscure piece of land which no civilized person had discovered so far and which for this precise reason was able to retain its elemental charm.

Gawd! This is fabulous! I will call it Paradise.[1] (pp.6-7)

The Minotaur, the title of the novel, too, is ecologically relevant. It is Caesar, the protagonist, who is aka Minotaur, in the novel. Minotaur, the mythological creature, is half-man and half-bull. Like majority of humankind, the writer reveals, Caesar has both the sides co-existing within him. He says that 'Minotaur' is the best myth conceived by the ancient mind to explain the bestiality existing within man. The bull represents power, masculinity and an irrational streak. The writer informs the readers that he is inspired by Picasso's *Guernica* and *Minotaur* Series and how in dealing with the legitimate opposition, a power-strung leader goes on a rampage like a bull and kill right and left under a lofty ideology. When a ruling humane philosophy becomes beastly and corrupt and loses its pristine appeal and justification, it is time it gets replaced by another, more compassionate version of another political ideology, aiming for rule over the hearts and minds of people. Minotaur always gets slaughtered at the altar of Time. Thus, the novel connects with the power discourses of the ancient and modern worlds and shows that people's verdict is the final arbiter, the last agent of bloody change.

Often in this novel, the reader comes across juxtaposition between the jungle- life and that of city-life. In Chapter 1, Caesar and his 20-men group discover the ancient ruined fort in an unexpected way which is massive and solid in structure with parapets and walls. He proclaims himself the new king of the territory that he calls 'Paradise' and all 20 members of the Group, his subjects. He goes to the extent of trampling his Rolex wristwatch and proclaims that time has stopped for all of them: Time stops for all of us. We are the new pioneers on a new mission. We do not need *their* time. (Sharma 7)

When at night time in his private chamber of the fort, Minotaurch feels the overwhelming presence of people who are trying to communicate with him, he wakes up aware of some invisible presence, the silence of centuries link him with early cavemen living thousands of years ago. He takes a sigh of relief for not being born in the ancient age when mortals were safe from all kinds of dangerous reptiles and creatures only if there was solidarity amongst the clan. At this point of time, he steps out in the central courtyard and is overawed by the majestic beauty of the night in the uninhabited land and like a transcendentalist finds the primeval spirits communing in the jungle at that time. Thus saying:

> He felt the cold on his bare skin and found it refreshing. The stars blinked at him and the rabbit in the moon gave one-toothed smile. Mellow dark pulsated around him in waves. The soothing moonlight illuminated his stony pathway. The fort was silhouetted in broad outlines against a silver-hued vastness of the sky. Jungle sounds came in filtered and subdued on the wings of the wind.
>
> He was overawed by the majesty of the night and the setting, so balming to his mind still rankling with the recent defeat and disgrace. The night looked so tender, soothing and mystical, different from the artifice of the city lit up by the sodium vapour lamps.
>
> *It is wonderful!This serenity and the tranquility! Primeval spirit of the jungle communing.*[2] (p.43)

In Chapter 2, the powerful Mark Livingstone, respected as the overall leader, by the Hararas who are scattered on all the islands, is all admiration for the rainfall that lends a surreal touch to the cloudy afternoon. Enchanted, he finds it musical lending harmony to the entire universe:

> Mark Livingstone was watching the rainfall in straight sheets. The dense rain and the greenery thick as a vertical column intermixed freely, the grayness of the rain lending a surreal touch to the

whole surroundings in the light-darkness of the afternoon. The heavy forest was dripping with rainwater. The curtain of the rain was moving fast from the dark skies to the damp wet floor of the brooding forest, a tall curtain joining heavens with the mother earth. Rains had always fascinated the white Harara. Rains that regenerated the forest and made it alive. The large settlement was being lashed furiously by the divine waters, producing its own harmony and sweet music.[3] (p.67)

Caesar projects himself as a true transcendentalist as he gets connected with history of the yore looking at the moon:

He stopped at the edge of the central courtyard and watched the ruins of the fort in the milky whiteness of the moonlight. Moon –the constant source of romance, poetry and philosophical speculations- the lonely wanderer in the blue infinite space, looking down upon the earthlings every night for millions of years, spreading cool light in the pathways of solitary wayfarers, cheering

them up from his empyrean
heights. The handsome
rugged moon, full-faced,
glowing as a lamp in the
dome, connecting him up with
the first inhabitants of the
earth, when no time existed! [4]
(p. 43)

Shaman, the ancient Harara, spreads a word that the
new chief is protected by the King Cobra and brings
luck to the tribe. He also informs the council that
every new chief has to undergo a test in which the
new chief has to go to the sacred temple in the
shadows of the Mount Ra, hundred and fifty miles
from the settlement for the fire test. If the fire-god
accepts him, the tribe also accepts him. He informs
them he will accompany the new chief to the sacred
temple as a guard to witness and that the new chief
has to submit to the authority of the fire god before
him. As Caesar is desperate to take the powerful
position of the tribal chief in order to win the loyalty
of the tribal clan, they start before dawn- the ancient
Harara and Constantine Caesar. The entire village of
Hararas gathers to bid the two farewell. As they forge
in the jungle, Caesar gets awed by the majesty of the
jungle- the entangling creepers and giant trees. He
finds the jungle alive with birdcalls. And he says:

It is like entering a different
world. Shadows and pale light
creating an illusionary zone.
The twisted pathways. The
slumbering jungle which
could be the grave for a lost
traveler with its criss-crossing
trails, dangerous animals and

biting insects, the slithering reptiles and poisonous berries....[5] (p.155)

He is enamored by the mystique of the forest, dwarfed by the huge trees –forgotten ages clinging to the two of them. He is sad and depressed to note that today human beings recognize no other values than power and wealth:

> Wilderness is a wrong term? Jungle has its own life. The first home to the human beings, plants and animals. Modernity and thirst for profits have destroyed this prime habitat. A priceless treasure, an album of the nursery of humankind when gods, giants, devils played with the highly- imaginative children, now lost and beyond retrieval for the adult rationalism of the modern, post-industrial world. An association beyond reclamation![6] (p. 157)

And later when he wakes up in the middle of the night and stretches himself, he calls the outdoor eternity, the balm for his spirit: The jungle calmed him up. His nerves were shot. The outdoors, the eternity just balmed his spirit. (Sharma 160)

In the meticulous handling of the narrative by the author, even Nature becomes a powerful character whether it is an account of the rain, the moon, the dark night or the Pacific

Ocean. In the following lines, the writer describes the Mexican desert as intimidating, one that spelt death to the wanderers who have lost their way and the ranch like a fortress:

In the blazing Mexico desert, the big ranch was a visual relief. The ranch was spread across acres of a wasteland dotted with cacti. The desert was immense and intimidating. It spelt death for those wanderers who had lost their way in its vastness. The tough terrain and conditions could drive anybody crazy in that land of sand except the locals or the Arabs. He remembered the lush forest, the dripping rain on the tree branches, the singing river, and the quiet blue Pacific Ocean. The rain has its music, pitter-patter, that sounds heavenly. The river and the big ocean have their own symphonies. He, deliberately, stopped thinking. The ranch was like a fortress. The outer parameters were electronically wired. Any contact with the live wires meant death. There were towers, search-lights and barbed wires. The desert was a suitable place for setting up the ranch for the would-be merchants of death. Any intruder or inquisitive inquirer could be seen from a mile in the flat featureless desert. Besides it could not afford any hiding place to any curious person. The ranch was a hundred miles away from the nearby town and the only means of transport was either a twin-engined plane or a sturdy land rover, and, both could be easily spotted by alert sentries. In the cold desert nights, the drone of a light plane or the spatter of a land rover could be heard easily. Besides that, there were landmines planted along the outer parameters that could blow any intruder into pieces. A squad of bloodhounds had the run of the place in the night.[7] (pp.118-119)

Natural mythology is being created and evolved through the variety of names designated by the writer. In Chapter 1, spiritual symbols are manifest in the sun,wind and rain: The chief deity, too, of the Harara tribe is the sun god, followed by the cobra and the fierce wind and rain gods. (Sharma 16) The names -Chameleon, Gorilla and Hydra-the local police are purely allegorical.

Gorilla, the six-feet two-inch tall, scar-faced giant, is nicknamed so for his massive physique and strength.

Chameleon is the vital link between Gorilla and the rest of the Hydra –the brilliant tactician, he was the ultimate and the champ in the words of the novelist. He was the dream of every spymaster. A master with disguises, fluent in tongues-ancient and modern, expert with explosives, a Masters from Harvard in Anthropology, he was taught the art of wrestling and the poisons by the Apaches, Kung Fu by Master Lee.

The members of Hydra, are the elite of the elite corps of the secret service, the ultimate killing machines, programmed to kill and survive in the most hostile climates, loyal only to their chief. They could remain without food, and water for many days, eating the natural resources available in their immediate local conditions-the all—terrain machines out to finish the job assigned at any cost. They were not afraid of any living things—fear was alien to their system—but only of their superior because failure meant death by the firing squad in the compound off the fortress- like headquarters of the Hydra- the secret police. They were not allowed to marry or drink. (Sharma 10)

Apart from this, when Caesar is being escorted by the ancient Harara for the fire test and at night time dozes off, he sees all dangerous animal species in his dream - the wolves prowling, growling and stalking him and vultures flying in the air. As he wakes up, sweaty and wet, he finds that he has been saved by the ancient Harara of the cobra who was now headless and writhing around in its last throes of death.

Another reference of the Nature being home to the dead souls and spirits is in Chapter 3.

It is the same night when Caesar is going to visit Mount Ra for the fire-test when after waking up from the dreadful dream, he witnesses two aborigines in loincloths and blood-shot eyes throwing a menacing look at him. Then other primitives too appear-short and stocky, well- built and well-muscled. Intimidated, he just prays and waits for the army of hunters to attack him. However, the night passes away making him feel that the jungle is playing tricks on him.

As the duo resume journey in the morning, Caesar recounts his experience of the night to the ancient Harara and he stops dead in the track and stares open-mouthed at Caesar. After thinking for a long time he tells Caesar that they were the spirits of Hararas:

> "You were lucky. They were the spirits of the Hararas. Forefathers. Going back   over the sleeping ages buried in the forest here. This land is sacred. Their bones are scattered here

about. Very few Hararas are permitted here by the law. Those who know the correct rituals and history are permitted. The men who lead good austere life. You saw the rare spectacle, which very few among us have witnessed. I knew one or two old men who had seen these holy spirits and communed with them. Their description fitted yours. I saw one or two of our sacred ancestors on my occasional visits here. And now, very soon, we will be entering a sacred place, the heart of the most holy place for us. You have to be cautious and respectful. Enter with the open mind of a child and you will get amply rewarded here." [8] (p.161)

Jungle is described as infested with supernatural elements and spirits. It's mystery and suspense ignites awe, wonder and fear in the protagonist.

Again after this there is beautiful description of the journey enroute Mount Ra that opens up new magical and mysterious realms before Caesar. He experiences an enchanting world of fluidity and musical silence and feels as if he is connected with the early stage of humanity:

"...Hoary ages, buried deep and preserved in the virgin forest, sprang up like a sturdy drawbridge, connecting up with the early childhood of humanity..." (Sharma 162)

A new sense of wonderment is rekindled in him that sheds off his skepticism and rationalism.

He thinks he is privileged in witnessing the sweet purity of a stage of the history denied to his peers and the breath-taking view is described in an artistically brilliant manner by the writer:

> Realms were opening up fast like a long hall of doors that led to more doors. Drenched in the mist, they walked quietly, afraid to disturb the sanctity of the place where the gods played with the early humans, the paths undulating among gigantic trees, the valleys rushing up and hills sloping down gently, a profundity deep and overwhelming, touching the very center of heart.

> The wind was caressing them and whispering melodious songs. The scent coming off from the flowers was invigorating and rejuvenating. Caesar felt lightness of being for the first time. Bliss overcame him. I want to die right here, in this unique state of blessedness!

> Almost drunk, he went on, greedily expecting more of this nectar, this manna, which he had never tasted before in any situation in his life—both as the President or as a commoner. His narrow heart expanded and felt full. He was utterly contented, despite the absence of power, wealth and prestige.

> I am at peace and happy.

And then the mist vanished equally suddenly, revealing a new vista of experience for him.

There, in full glory, was the Mount Ra. Kissed by the fluffy white clouds.

Splendid!

A breath- taking view. He was reminded of the White Mountains of Afghanistan. The Mount Ra sprang up abruptly in their field of vision: Huge, solid. Dominating the entire landscape: a range of tall mountains; the tallest one the sacred Mount Ra of the large tribe of the Hararas, its peak summit rising above other mounts, like a defiant gesture in massive stones sculpted by some invisible sculptor, to the empyrean heights of the blue vault. It was glittering in the cold rays of the sun; blanched white, the brilliance almost blinding.

A white diamond! [9] (pp.162-163)

Thus, any vigilant reader will not fail to find the strong ecological echoes that are recorded finely in the very fabric of the plot of this political text thereby making explicit the tacit message of the writer that Nature is something extremely important that needs to be preserved, treasured and treated with deference. Caesar himself calls the purity of Nature as nectar, as manna and feels invigorated, rejuvenated and full of bliss. He wants to die in that unique state of blessedness.

In a way, the writer wants to communicate that in order to develop human beings with the right mix of apathy and empathy, their proximity with Nature is utmost important that helps people in regaining their composure even in adverse circumstances. Wealth and power are not the only two things that bring solace. Nature brings peace and tranquility to modern human soul and mind. Propinquity to Nature is crucial to maintain the mental balance even during crises. For this reason, Nature needs to be conserved. Minotaur, a power-drunk dictator also finds ages buried in the misty forest, ruined fort and the tall pyramids. All of these have history concealed in them and ancient spirits of the Harara community are rich transcendental references.

Overall, *The Minotaur* is a rich and lyrical tribute to Nature and posits that it is the fountainhead of spiritualism, humanism and an ethical way of life (as represented by the simple lifestyle of the Hararas there).

Ultimately, as Constantine Caesar comes to learn before his tragic end that Nature can correct the mistakes of humankind and the code of the Hararas is an ideal one which integrates Nature and their life in a harmonious manner, those who try to tamper with such a natural order are bound to be vanquished.

Works Cited

(Note: The statements in italics are by the author- Sunil Sharma)

i)   Sharma, Sunil. *The Minotaur*. Jaipur: Book Enclave. 2009. pp. 6-7
ii) ibid p.43
iii) ibid p.67
iv) ibid p.43
v)   ibid p.155
vi) ibid p.157
vii) ibid pp.118-119
viii) ibid p.161
ix) ibid 162-163

Reconfiguring Ecofeminism: A Study of Women Characters in *Fire on the Mountain*

- Dr.Shweta Tiwari

Bio: Dr. Shweta Tiwari is currently working as an Assistant Professor in Amity Institute of English Studies and Research, Amity University, Uttar Pradesh. She is a gold medalist whose research papers have been published in several national and international journals. She also has various creative compositions to her credit that have found place in online forums like Women's Era, Muse India and Story Mirror

Abstract:

Ecofeminism claims that the oppression of women parallels the exploitation of nature and that the liberation of both is intertwined. The proponents of the movement derive their hypothesis from the value hierarchy and oppositional dualism rampant in the society. Ecofeminists intend to make people more perceptive to the subjugation of women and the consequent degradation of the environment but in doing so they reiterate numerous gender stereotypes. They believe that women by virtue of their gender are kinder than men and hence can relate more effectively to the 'mother' earth. This not only promotes the obsolete theory of biological determinism but also relegates women to the conventional role of caregiving. Also, the over-privileging of women's bodily functions such as menstruation, pregnancy and childbirth and its connection with the fertility of nature is like endorsing motherhood as the most important role in a woman's life. Through Anita Desai's *Fire on the Mountain*, the paper seeks to foreground theoretical loopholes in ecofeminism and that the relationship between women and nature is not absolute but ambivalent. The women characters in the novel straddle grey zones between the nature and culture binary based on which the paper argues for letting such ambivalence freely emerge in contemporary ecofeminist discourses.

Keywords: the Ambivalent, Culture, Dualism, Ecofeminism, Nature

Tracing the Trajectory

I know I am made from this earth, as my mother's hands were made from this earth, as her dreams came from this earth and all that I know, I know on this earth, the body of the bird, this pen, this paper, these hands, this tongue speaking, all I know speaks to me through this earth and I long to tell you, you who are earth too, and listen as we speak to each other of what we know: the light is in us. (Griffin, 227)

Coined by the French feminist Francoise d' Eaubonne, *eco-feminisme* began as an aesthetic-activist movement committed to examine the ramifications of sprawling urbanization on the ecosystem and women. An array of thinkers like Mary Daly, Carolyn Merchant and Karen J. Waren argued against Western anthropocentric/patriarchal environmental paradigms that reduce nature and living organisms into lucrative objects. They also identified women as agents of change on account of their being allegedly more empathetic than their male counterparts. Perceiving women and nature as mutually reinforcing entities may or may not be liberating but it is problematic.

The paper seeks to examine the lacunae in ecofeminist theory. On the basis of theoretical gaps it offers that the bond between women and nature is not absolute but ambivalent. It further situates ecofeminism in the Indian context and explores its reception by Indian English women writers with special emphasis on Anita Desai's *Fire on the Mountain*.

Interconnectedness between women and nature is embedded in historical, ideational and epistemological realms. From times immemorial, the reproductive capacity of a woman has been restricted within the confines of heteronormativity and motherhood across histories. Imposed gendered regulations led them to assume the role of a wife, breeder, feeder and ensurer of domestic tranquility. They continued to foster their male-dominated, ancestor-oriented families despite having limited resources. Over time, women began to be seen as a source of care-giving and sustainable development just like nature. Ideational or conceptual association between gender and ecology is grounded in the reductive model of binary opposition. Value dualism like reason-emotion, flesh-spirit, day-night, heaven-hell create hierarchy and make any pair oppositional rather than complimentary. In a patriarchal society, traits like strength, valour and aggression are related to men while women epitomize docility, benevolence and modesty. Thus, the reason behind equating culture with men and nature with women is not far to seek. Even the destructive forces of nature like storm, flood and volcanic eruptions are considered essential for keeping the ecology balanced just like a stern mother trying to discipline her child. Epistemic norms greatly influence what one regards as knowledge. Feminist epistemology states that knowledge was always created and disseminated from a masculine perspective therefore "various kinds of practical know-how and personal knowledge (knowledge that bears the marks of knower's biography and identity), such as the kind of untheoretical knowledge as mothers have of children, are undervalued when they are labeled "feminine" (Anderson,

50). Similarly, the belief that women are the most adversely affected by environmental degradation and they are closer to nature than men places them in an epistemologically privileged position. This implies that they have the authority to furnish as well as alter knowledge related to nature. In this case ecofeminism as Sandilands avows, "locates itself as a theory and movement which bridges the gap between feminism and ecology, but which transforms both to create a unified praxis to end all forms of domination" (3). Whether ecofeminism bridges the gap between feminism and environmental concerns or increases it, needs a closer analysis.s

Feminists dismiss the theory of biological determinism and contend that behavioral traits of both men and women are socio-culturally acquired. They exercise meticulous care while bringing within the scholarly ambit, women's bodily functions like menstruation and pregnancy lest they promote essentialism. Lee and Coen make a pertinent remark in this regard, "A prevailing fear among feminist scholars has been that, by studying uniquely female processes such as menstruation one might indirectly perpetuate the essentialist ideology which defines women as sex objects and reproducers, which sees women as being at the mercy of their biology" (6). On the contrary, ecofeminism is premised on the understanding that women-specific physiological functions such as ovulation, menstruation, pregnancy, labor pain and breast-feeding facilitate women to connect with 'mother' earth. Thus, drawing a comparison between life-giving ability of women and nature reinforces gendered stereotypes. Furthermore, ecofeminism fails to accommodate women whose sex, gender and sexual orientation does not align with socially-acceptable standards. This means that if menstruation and child-birth connect women to nature then trans-women and lesbians fall outside the domain of ecofeminism. The second predominant postulation of ecofeminism is that women and nature are united by a common oppressor. It cannot be denied that men have exploited women and nature for centuries but to believe that subjugation makes women more sensitive towards nature would be a sweeping generalization. Infact, it is like stating that being oppressed is a prerequisite to be perceptive to environmental degradation. Over-likening women to nature makes ecofeminism full of some glaring distortions. These include over-simplification of a global crisis, ignoring the participation of women in the destruction of natural habitats in the past as well as the present and undermining the contribution of men to conserve ecosystems. By privileging women over men, ecofeminists unwittingly create a model that bears a striking resemblance to patriarchy. Plumwood observes:

Perhaps the most obvious way to interpret ecofeminist argument is as one which replaces the masculine model of human character by a new feminine model. That is if the masculinizing strategy rejected the feminine character ideal and affirmed a masculine one for both sexes, this feminizing strategy rejects the masculine character ideal and affirms a feminine one for both sexes. (20)

Most of the works on the colonial era did not acknowledge women as historical or cultural subjects. The introduction of a postcolonial-feminist view point marked a radical departure from the past writings that were blind to the gender-class-caste nexus. However, ecofeminism and ecocriticism despite being relatively new concepts have betrayed traces of the Eurocentric worldview. Ecofeminist movement focused on socially advantaged females while largely excluding the concerns of 'poor' women hailing from 'lower-castes' in 'Third-World' countries. Indian women writers such as Mahasweta Devi, Kiran Desai, Arundhati Roy and social activists like Medha Patkar, C.K. Janu have raised the awareness of people about Postcolonial ecofeminism. However, even postcolonial ecofeminists remain unsuccessful in offering a viable blueprint for the conservation of the environment. For example, Vandana Shiva in her magnum opus launches a scathing attack on the western ideal of scientific reductionism but at the same time her over-romanticization of Third World women dilutes the potency of her argument. There are two main problems with the solution that Shiva proposes. Firstly, she glorifies subalterns (women, tribals, peasants) to an extent that it seems almost illogical. Secondly, she completely ignores the rural-urban and rich-poor divide among women of the Third World. The following excerpt highlights the lack of pragmatism in her proposition:

In contemporary times, Third World women, whose minds have not yet been dispossessed or colonised, are in a privileged position to make visible the invisible oppositional categories that they are custodians of. It is not only as victims but also as leaders in creating new intellectual ecological paradigms, that women are central to arresting and overcoming ecological crisis ... Third World women, and those tribals and peasants who have been left out of the processes of maldevelopment, are today acting as the intellectual gene pools of ecological categories of thought and action. Marginalisation has thus become a source of healing the diseased mainstream of patriarchal development. (44-45)

Women and Environmental Movements in India

Ecological activism also known as green politics dates back to the seventeenth century in India. This indicates that Indians were conscious of the overuse of renewable resources and deterioration of nature much before ecocriticism emerged as an academic discipline. Some of the country's local environmental movements include the

'Bishnoi Movement' (1730) in which hundreds of Bishnoi villagers hugged the trees and protested against their felling by the king's soldiers. The 'Chipko Movement' (1973) sprung from the awareness of the villagers that trees are important for soil conservation and reducing pollution. They too hugged the trees and fought for harvest rights. The movement created a global impact. The 'Save Silent Valley' (1978) was directed against the establishment of a hydroelectric project across the Kunthipuzha river that flows in the valley. Tribals of Bihar opposed the government's decision of planting profitable teak trees in place of natural Sal trees. This led to the 'Jungle Bachao Andholan' (1982). The 'Appiko Movement' (1983) witnessed people from all corners of Karnataka district who not only embraced trees to protect them but also carried out foot marches to promote afforestation. An objection by the locals to the construction of several dams on the Narmada river culminated in the 'Narmada Bachao Andholan' (1985). Another group of activists initiated the 'Tehri Dam Movement' (1990) to stop the construction of dams on Tehri river owing to a number of reasons like rapidly-submerging forest and seismic susceptibility of the region. Women were indispensable to these mobilizations but the reason behind their avid participation was more practical than sentimental. Much like men, women objected to anthropogenic activities, commercialization of forests and ruination of flora-fauna because nature served as a source of sustenance and livelihood for them.

Ecofeminism and India Women Writers

Women Writings in Indian English is a burgeoning literary area that integrates creativity with critical inquiry. Indian Women Writers have periodically responded to social issues that are inextricably linked with environmental concerns. Writer-activist, Mahasweta Devi's name in the field of ecofeminist writing needs no introduction. The sufferings of tribals and outcastes find an extensive documentation in Devi's novels such as *Hajar Churashir Ma* (Mother of 1084) and short stories like "Draupadi" and "Rudaali". Arundhati Roy is yet another noted writer who won the Booker Prize for her debut novel, *The God of Small Things*. She furnishes a severe criticism of Cartesian philosophy of dualism, state-sponsored development projects and nuclear testing in her writings. Likewise, a prolific poet and critic, Nandini Sahu deliberates on the relationship between woman and her surroundings in most of her poems. Her oft-quoted poetic narrative, *Sita: (A Poem)* is an ecofeminist rendering of the *Ramayana*. Contrary to the traditional characterization of Sita as a dutiful daughter and a self-negating wife, Sahu's Sita is bold and gallant who shares a mother-daughter relationship with the earth. The poet captures the descend of Sita back into the earth thus:

I was born of you, I wish to go back to you
The miracle happened, the redemption
emanated.
earth got divided at my feet, and a golden
throne arouse
 Mother Earth, the Ultimate Woman, arouse
 and took me in her lap ..." (108)

Padma Bhushan awardee (2014) Anita Desai was born to a German mother and a Bengali father in Mussorie in 1937. She is one of the most critically acclaimed Contemporary Indian English Women Writers. She has several novels to her credit, some of them include, *Cry, The Peacock* (1963), *Clear Light of Day* (1980), *The Village by the Sea*: *An Indian Family Story* (1982), *In Custody* (1984), *Fasting Feasting* (1999), *The Zigzag Way* (2004) and *The Artist of Disappearance* (2011). Desai has received Alberto Moravia Prize (2000), Benson Medal of Royal Society (2003) and Sahitya Akademi Fellowship (2007) for her literary marvels. She is also considered the pioneer of psychological novel in

Indian English. The internal conflicts, urges and experiences of the female protagonists of her novels are deeply influenced by nature. With a novel like *Fire on the Mountain* (1997) Desai has also cemented her reputation as an ecofeminist.

Fire on the Mountain is divided into three parts: "Nanda Kaul at Carignano", "Raka comes to Carignano" and "Ila Das leaves Carignano". The novel revolves around the chief character Nanda Kaul who savors a life of solitude in her widowed old age in Carignano, a placid but dilapidated house on a hilltop in Kasauli. Soon, her isolation is compromised by the arrival of her convalescing great-granddaughter, Raka. Like Kaul, Raka too eschews human contact and spends most of her time amid nature. In order to keep Raka engaged, Kaul fabricates a number of glorious stories about her past. The girl shows a brief interest in conversing with Kaul after which she gets desperate to escape. Kaul's serenity is further jeopardized by the entry of her childhood friend, Ila Das. A garrulous social reformer, Das embodies the antithesis of Kaul. After being disappointed in Raka, Kaul stops herself from talking extensively to Das which compels Das to return back to the village. Kaul heaves a sigh of relief at her friend's departure but her peace of mind is short-lived. She receives a call from a police inspector who informs her that Das has been raped and strangled on her way back home. Kaul is petrified to hear the news and wishes it to be a lie. She is shattered at the thought that her desire to be alone drove Das away in the dark of the night who would have otherwise been safe in her house. In the meanwhile, Raka calls her from outside to inform that she has set the forest on fire. The novel comes to an end with a thick smoke spiraling up over the mountain.

Women-Nature Bond in the Novel

The most obvious reading of a novel that foregrounds a connection between bounties of nature and actions of women is an ecofeminist one. An ecofeminist reading inevitably implies exploring the direct bond between women and their natural environment. In this case, *Fire on the Mountain* marks a departure. The women-nature relationship in the novel is equivocal, almost convoluted. Upon fulfilling her duties as a wife and a mother, Nanda Kaul chooses to live an isolated life on the ridge of a mountain in Kasauli. She shuns all kinds of human contact and relishes loneliness in her solitary abode called Carignano. Ecofeminist theory propounds that nature acts as a rejuvenating stimulant in the dreary lives of women. Desai's comprehensive description of the landscape surrounding Carignano and Kaul's own thought that "It was the place, and the time of her life— that she had wanted and prepared all her life" (3) tempts one to think that sumptuousness of nature gratifies her. However, it is soon informed that "What pleased and satisfied her so, here at Carignano was its barrenness" (4). Kaul also dismisses the presence of apricot tress and iris clumps in the vicinity as "incidental, almost unimportant" and a hoopoe feeding its nestlings as "a sight that did not fill her with delight" (5). This is in contrast to the presupposition that women essentially rejoice each and every aspect of nature. Also, her repeated reference to sterility, stillness and desolation is opposed to fecundity and life generally associated with women and nature. For example, she fancies to "merge with the pine tree and be mistaken for one. To be a tree, no more, no less was all she was prepared to undertake" (4). In this regard, S. Indira opines, "Nanda's sense of identification with the pine trees suggests her desire for absolute stillness and withdrawal from life" (97).

The Hindu tradition talks about four age-based stages of a human life: scholar, householder, retired and ascetic. The last stage is marked by renunciation of material life and worldly ties in order to attain an introspective life. People in pursuit of isolation and spirituality usually migrate to remote hermitages or boarding houses located away from the city-din. Likewise for Kaul phone calls and letters are "unwelcome intrusion and distraction" (3). Kaul's occasional brooding over her past reveals that her life as a wife of a university Vice-Chancellor and a mother to several children had been quite busy. She divided her time between "mending clothes, sewing on strings and buttons and letting out hems" and "instructing the servant girl", (19). She was extolled by "the wives and daughters of the lecturers and professors over whom her husband ruled" for being adept at house-keeping. One of the main reasons behind associating women and nature is also because both of them are 'productive'. By productive it is meant that women not only gather and eat what grows in nature but they also tender nature to grow them. After performing household chores, supervising servants, hosting her husband's guests and nurturing her children for a considerable part of her life, Kaul completes her duties and in her old age takes refuge in "the sound of cicadas, and the pines, the sight of this gorge plunging, blood-red, down to the silver plain (21). Thus, one infers that it is natural for her to willingly lead a secluded life, post-retirement. Ecofeminists affirm that nature is a source of both leisure and escape for women. The readers are deluded to believe the same about Nanda Kaul until she reveals the actual reason behind her living in denial. Towards the end of the novel, Kaul recalls the excruciating emotional deprivation she suffered due to the extra-marital affair of her husband and her ungrateful children for whom she felt no affection or fondness. Thus, Kaul's guarded existence in a forsaken corner is more enforced than voluntary:

Nor had her husband loved and cherished her and kept her like a queen— he had only done enough to keep her quiet while he carried on a lifelong affair with Miss David, the mathematics mistress, whom he had not married because she was a Christian but whom he had loved, all his life loved. And her children− the children were all alien to her nature. She neither understood nor loved them. She did not live here alone by choice− she lived here alone because that was what she was forced to do, reduced to doing. (158)

Raka's link with nature is much more complex than Kaul and her character defies an easy categorization. She is sent to her great-grandmother to recover back her health after a near-fatal attack of typhoid. The girl is nothing like her name which means the moon. On the contrary, she is described as "one of those dark crickets that leap up in fright but do not sing, or a mosquito, minute and fine, on thin, precarious legs" (43). Raka's father is a diplomat posted in Geneva thus it becomes evident that she hails from an affluent family. However, it is soon revealed that he is a drunkard who thrashes his wife violently and has numerous affairs outside marriage. Raka recalls cowering in fear at her father's abusive behavior as a young girl. Consequently, the girl grows up hating her father and pitying her bed-ridden mother. Raka mostly avoids talking to Kaul but eagerly chatters with the cook, Ram Lal who informs her about the "big party of the summer season" (73). Though he confirms that post-colonial army revelry is quite different from the ball dance of the colonizers yet curiosity drives Raka to see for herself, the said night of carousing. The scene of the cantonment party leaves her flabbergasted, "There was no vision of kings and queens in a rosy court. To the heated drumming of the band, madmen and rioters leapt, bowed, swayed and jigged, costumes flying, paper horns blowing. It was lunacy rampant. Raka held her head between her hands, she thought it would crack in two" (75). Raka is appalled at the sight of a "woman with a bucket on her head" who "laughed in bubbles of blood", a figure with "skull and crossbones in white upon his chest", an "outsized monkey with a stiff, curling tail" and a "lady mouse" who "was being chased by a man who had his hair combed down over his eyes and wore a scarf around his neck like a noose before it is tightened" (76). The party represents the material world which reminds Raka of the brutalities of her father and mental wreckage of her mother. Thus, Raka's avid involvement with the landscape, valley, sunrise, trees and animals is indicative of her seeking in nature a break from her dreadful past. Just when the readers become confident that unlike Kaul, Raka is a recluse by choice and feels immense exhilaration in the lap of nature, she sets the forest on fire. Her act of burning the forest is open to multiple interpretations. The charred trees and burnt Pasteur Institute for psychiatric patients, a colonial bastion for curing mental disorders symbolize Raka's smashing traditional conformities, existing systems and sites of male violence. The fire can be seen as an objective correlative to Raka's distraught emotions and inner dissension. It can also be considered a way by which Raka tries to awaken Kaul's sensibilities that by distancing others, she was rejecting a part of herself that secretly craved for companionship. All the above elucidations share one thing in common, i.e. Raka's relationship with nature vacillates between constructive and destructive.

The presence of Ila Das, a piano teacher turned social welfare worker in the neighboring villages is short yet crucial to the plot. Das is Kaul's childhood friend who once belonged to a thriving family but is now forced to eke out a meager living due to her wastrel brothers. She is projected as a diminutive and ludicrous old lady whose greatest tragedy in life is her voice. Kaul loathes Das's screeching voice which the former feels is "like a long nail frantically scratching at the glass pane, or a small child gone berserk and prattling on and on in a voice no one could hear without cringing" (22). Upon knowing the arrival of Raka at Carignano, Das decides to meet both the women but even her walk up the mound is full of "Whooping and hooting, munching and mooing of schoolboys" (118). Das may be caricatured for comical effect but she supplies the most important insights about human life in the novel. Das is deprived of her share in the family's wealth and is also given the responsibility of her ailing mother but she is not an escapist like Kaul. Her becoming a social worker further highlights that apart from personal relations, she believes in community service also. She rues, "'how helpless our upbringing made us, Nanda. We thought we were being equipped with the very best—French lessons, piano classes, English governess—my, all that only to find it left us helpless, positively *handicapped* (139). The rant is suggestive of the snobbery of upper-class women who fail to inculcate in them humanity and ethical values. Das's character is explicitly located at the cusp of nature and culture. She oscillates between both the worlds but does not assimilate in either. On the one hand, she fulfils her obligation as a social worker by stopping the child marriage of Preet Singh's daughter and on the other she thinks about being a peasant and "Grow a pumpkin vine, keep a goat, pick up kindling in the forest of fire" (139). On the same night, while returning back from Kaul's house Das is murdered and raped by an enraged Preet Singh. Her reformist venture culminates in a painful death, "Crushed back, crushed down into the earth, she lay raped, broken, still and finished (156). Das's effort to impart education to village women and interference in customary practices like child marriage (nature's attempt to enter into the domain of culture) disturbs the established patriarchal order of the village and is met with a macabre end (culture's infliction of violence upon nature). This episode is significant as it brings out yet another ambivalence in women-nature relationship. A common parallel drawn between women and nature is that both succumb to male forces, silently. Das does not let Preet Singh overpower her immediately. She staggers but retaliates, "She struggled, chocking, trying to stretch and stretch and stretch that gasp till it became a shout, a shout that the villagers would hear ..." (155). Nagpal rightly observes, "The woman protagonists are portrayed as victims of an aberrant urban milieu, patriarchal family structures and bourgeoisie, bureaucratic, imperialist, colonized social scenario. It is in this context that the characters are in a state of revolt, despondency, morbidity and are driven to grapple with duality, fragmentation." (49)

Conclusion

Fire on the Mountain disrupts the nature-culture dualism in favor of foregrounding a more realistic and dynamic relationship between women and nature. The characterization of women in the novel urges the readers to look at them as multifaceted beings who perform numerous roles and thus possess pluralistic opinions on environment and its conservation which do not necessarily have to be 'feminine'. The ecofeminist assumption that women are more 'connected' to nature is problematic because interlocking system like food chains and food web connect each and every living creature to nature. The second aspect of their being more 'sensitive' needs a closer analysis as it perpetuates same gender stereotypes that are vehemently opposed by the feminists. It is also important to note that as academically accomplished, professional women residing in urban centers, millennial women have as much right over cities as nature. Therefore, it is obstructionist to align women to nature without reflecting on the gender-class-caste complex that moulds their experiential and ecological perspectives. Environmentalist, ecocritics and ecofeminists intend to devise ethical guidelines to promote a cleaner and greener environment. The endeavor might succeed in stirring the consciousness of people and producing the desired result but an uncritical privileging of women's bodily functions to justify the hypothesis of ecofeminism certainly needs a revision.

Works Cited

Primary Source

Desai, Anita. *Fire on the Mountain*. New Delhi: Vintage Books, 2012. Print.

Secondary Sources

Anderson, Elizabeth. "Feminist Epistemology: An Interpretation and a Defense." *Hypatia: A Journal of Feminist Philosophy* 10.3 (1995): 50-84. Print.

Biehl, Janet. *Rethinking Ecofeminist Politics*. Boston: South End Press, 1991. Print.

Gadgil, Madhav and Ramachandra Guha. *Ecology and Equity*: *The Use and Abuse of Nature in Contemporary India*. New Delhi: Oxford UP, 1995. Print.

Griffin, Susan. *Women and Nature: The Roaring Inside Her*. New York: Harper and Row, 1978. Print.

Indira, Sivanna. *Anita Desai as an Artist: A Study in Image and Symbol*. New Delhi: Creative Books, 1994. Print.

Kaur, Gurpreet. "Women, Animals and Violence: Anita Desai's *Fire on the Mountain* and Lee Yew Leong's "Honey, I'm Off To Be A Jellyfish Now." *The Journal of Ecocriticism*: *A New Journal of Nature, Society and Literature* 8.1 (2018): 1-9. Print.

Lee, Janet and Jennifer Saaser-Coen. *Blood Stories: Menarche and the Politics of the Female Body in*

Contemporary U.S. Society. New York: Routledge, 1996. Print.

Nagpal, B.R. "Existential-Spiritual Quest in Anita Desai's *Fire on the Mountain.*" *Roman Critical Context*: *Anita Desai's Fire on the Mountain*. Kolkata: Roman Books, 2014. 49-60. Print.

Sahu, Nandini. *Sita (A Poem)*. New Delhi: The Poetry Society of India, 2015. Print.

Sandiland, Kate. "Ecofeminist and Its Discontent: Notes Towards Political Diversity." *The Trumpeter*: Journal *of Ecosophy* 8.2 (1991): 90-96. Print.

Shiva, Vandana. *Staying Alive: Women, Ecology and Survival in India*. New Delhi: Kali for Women, 1988. Print.

Plumwood, Val. "Women, Humanity and Nature." *Radical Philosophy* (1998):16-24. Web. 21 June 2019.

An Ecocritical study of Amitav Ghosh's *The Hungry Tide*

- Tanmay S. Bhamre

Bio: **Tanmay Sunil Bhamre** is a student of English Literature and Economics at B.K. Birla College, Kalyan. He has won several awards in debate, elocution and other literary competitions. He is an avid reader and skater.
Correspondence Address –
A-1/502, Mangala-Park, Khadakpada, Kalyan, Maharashtra, India.
Phone: 7900122414 / 9892201463

Email: tanmay.bhamre1@gmail.com

"Ether, air, fire, water, earth, planets, all creatures, directions, trees and plants, rivers and seas, they are all organs of God's body. Remembering this, a devotee respects all species."

– Srimad Bhagavatam (2.2.41)

Abstract:

Environmental concerns and theories may be common to all countries, but issues vary in magnitude, limits, technicalities, standards, and impacts from country to country. Copying policies and modules from other countries and posting them just as it is on the face of India's environment is fruitless. The implementation of environmental plans is the biggest challenge in India. Jnanpith Award winner, Amitav Ghosh is one of the very few writers who make evident how sensitive it is for an agency to administer environmental policies. In many of his works, he highlights the centrality of environmental concerns and their profound connection with literature. Set on a remote island in the Sunderbans, the *Hungry Tide* by Amitav Ghosh explores the precarious life and struggle of people against shifting islands, predators and repercussions of past environmental policies gone wrong. This paper attempts to analyze how Amitav Ghosh weaves the remembered past and the witnessed present together and to scrutinize how the eco-critical perspective radiates in the novel.

Keywords: Environmentalism, Conservationism, Eco-Criticism, Hunger.

An Eco-Critical Study of Amitav Ghosh's The Hungry Tide.

Amitav Ghosh is one of the leading Indian English authors. He writes in tune with global change, multicultural surroundings, cosmopolitanism and philosophical doctrine of environmentalism, and he has not neglected to depict in his novels the darker sides of India. His novel, *The Hungry Tide*, depicts the sad tale of agonies of the low-class immigrants and the harsh realities of the life of the Sundarbans. The book is set in one of the most dynamic and fascinating ecological systems of the world and expounds the wrath of nature and human frailty at the hands of nature. The author explores human cost of environmental conservation and subaltern stories which would otherwise be forgotten.

The story unravels through the eyes of two characters, Kanai Dutt and Piyali Roy (Piya), who are visitors to the

Sunderbans. Kanai is a successful translator from Delhi and Piya is a cetologist who is on her crusade to research a rare Irrawaddy Dolphin, *Orcaellabrevirostris*. Kanai along with Fokir, an illiterate fisherman and Kusum, helps Piya in her research. The story is set in Lusibari, located in the immense labyrinth of tiny islands of Sunderbans. Kanai explores the history of the area and Piya journeys through the present. Ghosh unravels the threads of the story by contrasting and jumping back and forth to Kanai and Piya's narratives. He underlines the problems of identity and culture in the novel and reconciles these with environmental issues.

Amitav Ghosh has visited Sunderbans numerous times. He paints a vivid picture of the tide country before us. He describes:

"There are no borders here to divide fresh water from salt, river from sea. The tides reach as far as three hundred kilometers inland and every day thousands of acres of forest disappear underwater only to re-emerge hours later... When the tides create new land, overnight mangroves begin to gestate, and if the conditions are right they can spread so fast as to cover a new island within a few short years. A mangrove forest is a universe unto itself... Mangrove leaves are tough and leathery, the branches gnarled foliage often impassably dense. Visibility is short and the air still and fetid ... Every year dozens of people perish in the embrace of that dense foliage, killed by tigers, snakes and crocodiles." (Ghosh 7)

Sunderbans have an ever-changing topography. Powerful currents reform the land every day when thousands of acres of forest disappear underwater. Hours later, it re-emerges. This theme of transformation is beautifully described in the lines:

"But here, in the tide country, transformation is the rule of life: rivers stray from week to week, and islands are made and unmade in days. In other places forests take centuries, even millennia, to regenerate; but mangroves can recolonize a denuded island in ten to fifteen years. Could it be the very rhythms of the earth were quickened here so that they unfolded at an accelerated pace?" (Ghosh 186)

Amrita Banerjee reflects in her paper - *Hostile spaces, Gender Response: A reading of The Hungry Tide* that:

"The Hungry Tide provides an insider's view of the patterns of survival in one such hostile space 'India's doormat', the Sunderbans." [2]

For people, survival is an everyday struggle- men venture far out into the rivers in order to fish which a very risky task, given the predators lurking in the unknown. They live under constant threat of tidal floods and attacks by predators:

"Like the big bed, it was enclosed in a permanent canopy of heavy netting. Mosquitoes were the least of the creatures this net was intended to exclude; its absence, at any time, night or day, would have been an invitation for snakes and scorpions to make their way between the sheets. In a hut, by the pond, a woman was even said to have found a large dead fish in her bed. This was a koimachh, or tree perch, a species known to be able to manipulate its spiny fins in such a way as to drag itself overland for short distances. It had found its way into the bed only to suffocate on the mattress." (Ghosh 74)

Environmental issues caused by human activities have become increasingly serious in recent times. Interdisciplinary Studies in Literature and Environment can foster good governance. Literature, since its inception, has depicted nature in one way or other. Thus, eco-critical study has been a major catalyst in promoting Green-governance in 21st century. The novel explores humanism and environmentalism in contrast with each other and the conflict of interests that arises from them. Powerful forces of nature render human frail but the human settlement in places meant for flora and fauna also harms nature. He uses powerful imagery to not only highlight the fascinating features but also the devastating effects of nature. Animals are more sensitive than humans. Our planet is warming faster than any rate seen in the past 10,000 years. These fluctuations make it harder for animals to adapt to new patterns. Mangroves, in particular, are very sensitive to shifts in climatic conditions and habitat loss. Ample evidence projecting the reduction in the natural biodiversity is found in the Red List of Threatened from the International Union for Conservation of Nature (IUCN). As of 2017, the list highlights 87,967 species, of which 25,062 are in danger of extinction, mangroves being home to a third of them. The hungry tides in the novel are portrayed as corollary of degradation of mangroves, which are habitats for seabirds, amphibians, and aquatic animals. This is true. The destruction of mangroves makes an area prone to severe tidal floods. City of Mumbai has a same troubled relationship with the environment and it has lost around 40 percent of its mangrove forest cover in recent decades, which results in severe water-clogging and floods in surrounding area during the monsoon season. The situation has escalated in past few monsoon cycles- in 2018 the sea spew out 2, 15,000 kilo grams of trash back at Mumbai. People often underestimate mangroves which could provide multiple ecosystem services that support, protect and enhance the economies and livelihoods of coastal communities. This human hunger has given rise to ravenous wrath of the nature.

Ghosh portrays this hunger in a verbatim sense. This hunger has plurality of layers. It is both literal and metaphoric in nature. It refers to the flustering emotional tide which engulfs every character in the novel. Almost every major character is consumed by their hunger or desire. The romantic interweaving of the characters, by the author, shows us that hunger is present in every human heart. It is also symbolized in the perpetual flow of tides, which ravenously submerge miles of land every day. The tidal movements add fuel to the narrative; it brings people together and forces them apart. He displays the element of hunger in the daily struggle of islanders against the devastating environment. The story unravels from two perspectives of many different characters and their inner struggles. Through second hand information the author paints a picture of hunger and starvation before us. Kanai's ideological aunt and uncle (Nirmal and Nilima) are long time settlers of Sunderbans. When they first arrive in Lusibari they observe:

"The destitution of the tide country was such as to remind them of the terrible famine that had devastated Bengal in 1942 – except that in Lucibari hunger and catastrophe were a way of life. [...]The settlers were mainly farmers but hunger drove them to hunting, fishing and honey collecting. The result was disastrous – many died of drowning; many were killed by tigers and crocodiles: No day seemed to pass without the news of someone being killed by a tiger, a snake or a crocodile." (Ghosh 67)

In the novel, it is depicted that the tigers of the Sunder bans have developed an odd taste for human flesh – primarily due to human encroachment in the area. They are feared predators. Villagers have their own complex theories about the tiger attacks – some say that the corpses of killed refugees that had floated through the water had given them a taste for human flesh. Others argue that human encroachment has annoyed and provoked tigers into attacking humans and that is how they developed a taste for human flesh. Divya Anand elaborates this in paper- *Words on Water: Nature and Agency in Amitav Ghosh's the Hungry Tide*. She says-

"If it is the tiger's hunger that keeps encroachers at bay and protects the forests, it is hunger that drives men into illegally entering the forests." [3]

The author intricately weaves the remembered past and the witnessed present together; it is seen when Kanai reads extracts from his uncle's journals which describe the history and the struggles of first inhabitants of the area. The story is set against the backdrop of a real historic migration case, refugee resettlement and consequent violence and bloodshed on the island of Morichjhapi. The Morichjhapi incident in the *Hungry Tide* is depicted through Nirmal's diary. Sunderbans is home to the Royal Bengal Tigers. Highly revered and hugely feared, these beautiful creatures are at a point of extinction. Due to constant international pressure, the Bengal Government declared Morichjhapi as a tiger reserve and began to evict people. Many died resisting. This left the inhabitants with a notion that the government cares more about the tigers than the people. Ghosh blends this historic struggle well into the plot. The condition of people living in the area is much inferior to animals and is best highlighted when Kusum agonizes:

"Who are these people, I wondered, who love animals so much that they are willing to kill us for them [...] it seemed to me that this whole world had become a place of animals, and our fault, our crime, was that we were human beings, trying to live as human beings always have, from the water and the soil." (Ghosh 261)

Marooned by a dam, displaced twice and blazoned as Maoist sympathizers, Malkangiri's tribal people share same fate today. Located in the highlands around the Balimela Reservoir in Odisha'sMalkangiri district, tribals are caught in the crossfire between Maoists and the Border Security Force. They felt isolated and neglected. But things are turning around for the tribals with implementation of schemes like *Swabhiman Anchala*. The Odisha government now is determined to take development to the remotest parts of the area to compensate for the decades of alienation. This should also be contributed to the writers and journalists who spend years of hardship in order to bring such stories in light. Thus, writers build the understanding of environmental issues not only by drawing upon and tendering to the environmental social sciences, but also by linking the social and natural sciences. Amitav Ghosh is one of them.

He understands the sensitivity of environmental policies. He narrates stories from subaltern perspectives – their interactions with their environment, state, predators, economic hardships and each other. In the *Hungry Tide*, he highlights that poor implementation of development and conservation policies not only foster conflicts between the communities and the protected area framework but has also increased the justification of social exclusion and environmental degradation, which often adds fuel to the fire of Naxalite movement. New ways of governing with respect to the environment have significant consequences for conservation practice. Greater awareness of the grass root situation can help conservation managers and scientists more effectively participate in governance processes. For conservationists it is also crucial to identify the competing political ideologies underlying this process. One must consider the diverse interests that play a major role in shifting patterns of local nature–societal interaction which configures a complex politicized environment before implementing conservationist policies. He manages to illuminate this notion through the character of Kanai Dutt, who in a fiery exchange of words with Piya, says-

"Because it was people like you who made a push to protect the wildlife here, without regard for the human costs. And I'm complicit because people like me [...] have chosen to hide these costs, basically in order to curry favor with their Western patrons. It's not hard to ignore the people who're dying—after all, they are the poorest of the poor." (Ghosh 248)

As an anthropologist turned writer, Ghosh innately desires to improve the conditions in the tide country. It is not only a fictional story of the natives and their surrounding environment, but also an exploration of the character's hearts. Every character strives to have a deep relationship, either with their surroundings or each other. This is demonstrated by Dr.S.Alexander and K.A. Kasthuri in their paper, *Ecocriticism in Amitav Ghosh's the Hungry Tide*:

"When Piya and Fokir are trapped by the cyclone, it is the extreme desperation and fight for survival that brings them together. Piya begins with a mistranslation of the people and environment around her and proceeds to represent a movement towards equality between elite and subaltern culture. Ghosh wants to suggest if the world is to see the positive change through social anthropology, there is the need to promote such cross-cultural relations. This fact that the present study detects mental agony of the inhabitations living in a fragile ecosystem is information about the condition of the people, and the present generation can take up fruitful steps to help improve the situation of Tide country." [4]

The relationship between Piya and Fokir is very riveting (especially in contrast of her relationship with Kanai). Despite the language barrier they share close moments. For me, their inability to speak to one another is a necessary issue in the book because it shows that love and compassion can cross any barriers. She is attracted to him because of his innate relationship with his surroundings and ability to locate dolphins which Piya is so eager to study. Her character is depicted to romanticize the connection of locals and their surrounding environment. But the tiger killing incident in the novel brings out the contrasting cultures of both of them. This ongoing conflict with the humans for their survival is resulting in decline of tiger populace. Due to lack of food, shelter and water, tigers are leaving their natural habitats and going to human settlements in search of resources. The author compels readership into a dilemma as to who is actually intruding whose space? People who came to the land, they are trying to live, trying to survive, just like Sir Daniel Hamilton who aspired to build a new society in the tide country. They have no other option than to kill the tiger in order to stay alive, which is exactly what the tiger is trying to do - Survive. The tigers were already there, that's a fact, but so were people until they were driven away because of natural disasters. Who does the tide country, after all, belong to? It is here the emotional connections of Piya and Fokir divides. She considers the act of killing a tiger as cruel and inhumane and hopes that Fokir might oppose the tiger killing. But she discovers that Fokir is also involved in the act, which brings out major societal differences of both the characters and makes Piya wonder whether she has misinterpreted Fokir. She idealised him as a man sensitive to his surroundings and is shaken to the core when Fokir gets involved in the act. In turn, Ghosh exposes the unwanted complexities existing in human relationships. Dr. S. Alexander and K.A. Kasthuri beautifully describe the author's motive behind the two characters. In their paper, they state-

"Ghosh wants to suggest that if the people of both privileged and impoverished backgrounds are united, then there will be prosperous future for the world's poor. The relationship between Piya and Fokir symbolizes the union between two." [4]

Through the characters of Piya and Fokir, I believe the author asks us not to judge any person harshly, as he or she are only a result of their societal construct and that one must listen to others with humility and regard. The character of Fokir is very intriguing. He is nature lover and although he is illiterate by western standards of education, he shows very strong philosophical and moral foundation of values. Author also contrasts Piya's Western scientific training against Fokir's natural instincts. He knows the river system quite well and in fact belongs to the flux of rivers. He is depicted as an outcast - a Fakir, who has no material needs and no longings and feels free in the natural environment. In the end, he dies a noble death. To honor Fokir's death, Piya undertakes a conservation project with a grass-root level participation. Nilima helps Piya in her endeavour. Community based conversation is a significant thing for sake of both - humans and animals. Author manages to highlight that if someone (like Piya in the novel) is ready to undertake a conservation project, they should apply indigenous people's knowledge in tandem with modern technologies.

Ghosh warns his readers of the anthropocentric approach of humans towards nature. He believes man and nature can co-exist together, only if a harmonious balance is maintained. He makes us 'conscious' of our actions. Gaurav Mishra in his paper - *Ecological Vision Regarding the Sundarbans:*

Towards an Ecocritical Reading of Amitav Ghosh's the Hungry Tide, rightly observes that –

"Through this ecologically conscious novel, Ghosh has presented a true picture of the real world where humanity has been perpetually losing its basic tenets. Since time immemorial, man has given every effort to make him stand apart from other animals, and has established the base for humanity. But today's anthropocentric civilization is unable to carry all of those humanitarian beliefs forward. Man's anthropocentric attitude has been motivating him to bring into play every other entity to fulfill his own purposes." [5]

Theme of woman empowerment has appeared in almost every fictional work of Amitav Ghosh and *the Hungry Tide* is no different. Ghosh's women characters challenge the traditional stereotypical gender roles of women in society. One such character, which seems to have vowed to break the gender stereotype, is that of Piyali Roy. She is an American citizen of Indian origin who bravely ventures into the unknown. She goes where her work takes her, with courage and determination, come what may. She carries state-of-the-art equipment for her research work and the author symbolizes the themes of globalization and modernization in her. Through her character, he advocates that we can utilize technology not only for destruction of environment, but also for constructive usages. He reminds us that humans are not the only species who have the right to live and that animals also love and feel pain: what animal rights advocates call *Anti-Speciesism*. This moral lesson if best exemplified when Piya says:

"Just suppose we crossed that imaginary line that prevents us from deciding that no other species matters, except ourselves. What will be left then?

Aren't we alone enough... once we decide we can kill off other species, it'll be people next- who are poor and unnoticed" (Ghosh 249)

Author narrates the plight of the women through Nilima's eyes, Kanai's aunt. She, unlike her husband Nirmal, accepts the actual situation, the reality and does not spend her days dreaming and lamenting how world should be. Rather she strives hard to improve the conditions of women. With her tenacity and stubborness, she erects Badabon Development Trust to help the poor people providing those basic amenities of food, shelter, safe drinking water and electricity; it grows to become an organisation which is widely renowned as an ideal model of NGO working in rural India. Fishing is a risky task and whenever men venture out into the rivers women fear whether they will ever see their husbands again or not. She dedicates her entire life to alleviate the conditions of women and men of the tide country and to build-

"A place where no one would exploit anyone and people would live together without petty social distinctions and differences, where men and women could be farmers in the morning, poets in the afternoon and carpenters in the evening." (Ghosh 46)

Nature is portrayed as a social leveler by the author. When the tide comes, it irons out all hierarchies constructed by humans. When nature wrecks havoc it affects every person equally. All societal constructed boundaries of class, gender, language and caste disappear when nature strikes. Apart from this the storm at the end of the novel, victimizes human beings and animals equally. Nature, therefore, is portrayed as impartial, the great disregarder of social status and pretensions.

As the narrative unfolds, two issues emerge – the issue of climate change and the immigrant problem and, in many cases, their intertwined connection. This novel is also a wakeup call to all of us. It is to remind us that the climate change problem is real and that we have to play our part in fighting it. In a way, this fictional work by Amitav Ghosh strives to support Aldo Leopold's view regarding environmental conservation. Mr. Leopold in his book *A Sand County Almanac*, states –

"Conservation is a state of harmony between men and land. By land is meant all of the things on, over, or in the earth. Harmony with land is like harmony with a friend; you cannot cherish his right hand and chop off his left. That is to say, you cannot love game and hate predators; you cannot conserve the waters and waste the ranges; you cannot build the forest and mine the farm. The land is one organism. Its parts, like our own parts, compete with each other and co-operate with each other. The competitions are as much a part of the inner workings as the co-operations. You can regulate them—cautiously—but not abolish them." (Leopold 145)

The traditional, colonial narratives of the tide country are revitalized and rewritten by the author in a new light. He manages to do so by infusing the novel with elements from other disciplines such as anthropology, demography, sociology, archaeology, human geography, etc. He advocates that countries should not cling to models of economic development that marginalize the local and subaltern in favor of the metropolitan, buttressing the best and ruthlessly exploiting the worst. He compels the readership to ponder over how one should position oneself in relation to today's geopolitical inequalities and the intricacies of environmental ethics and politics.

Reading *the Hungry Tide*, in a way, is like reading the tide country.

Conclusion

The eco-critical and post-colonial purview of this novel has been extolled and analyzed by many critics such as Divya Anand, Nazia Hassan, and Dr.Alexander. This paper is a humble attempt to focus only on one of the many aspects which Amitav Ghosh blends into the novel. The novel is not only rich from an environmental perspective but also from the feminist and post-colonial view-point. *The Shadow Lines, the Calcutta Chromosome, in an Antique Land, the Glass Palace, the Hungry Tide* and *Sea of Poppies,* all these books portray women as strong allegorical figures. But his literary mission behind writing *the Hungry Tide* is to express his concern over the environment and to immortalize the historical events which would otherwise be forgotten. He beautifully constructs nature before us by interweaving past events and experiences with present issues of migration and collapse in cultures. He highlights that the immediate requisite is to build a future which fabricates a balance between man and his surroundings. In dichotomy of eco-critical, feminist and postcolonial theory, Amitav Ghosh does not offer a distinct solution, he only demonsrates the dangers and difficulties which arise from the conflict of interests. In a way, Ghosh is like a doctor from the medieval ages who at the early stages of medicine, could only understand the nature of the disease but could not suggest any solid, panacean cure. By describing the Sundarbans as an environmentally sensitive area, he tells us that it is difficult to address the planet's ecological problems without an in-depth evaluation of human and cultural issues linked to natural ecosystems. Green governance, in today's age, is the dire need of the hour. It would not be erroneous to conclude that this genre-bending book goes beyond the doomsday, dystopian version of literature on climate change.

Works Cited

1. Ghosh, Amitav. The Hungry Tide. London: HarperCollins, 2004. Print.
2. Banerjee, Amrita. "Hostile spaces, Gender Response A reading of The Hungry Tide." *Quest Journals,* 2011.
3. Anand, Divya. "Words on Water: Nature and Agency in Amitav Ghosh's The Hungry Tide." *Concentric: Literary and Cultural Studies.*, 2008, pp 15.
4. Alexander, S., & Kasthuri, K.A. "Ecocriticism in Amitav Ghosh's The Hungry Tide." *Research Journal of English Language and Literature,* 2016, pp 176-177.
5. Mishra, Gaurav. "Ecological Vision Regarding the Sundarbans: Towards an Ecocritical Reading of Amitav Ghosh's The Hungry Tide." *Impression Journal of English Studies*, 2019, pp 2.
6. Leopold, Aldo. A Sand County Almanac and Sketches Here and There. New York: Oxford Univ. Press, 1949, pp 145.

Memoir by Roula Pollard

Bio: Roula Pollard is a Greek poet, writer, translator, literary promoter, peace and environmental activist whose work has been published in four poetry collections. She has also published short stories and essays and participated in international poetry festivals. She has received international poetry awards and diplomas and her work has been translated into eight languages. She writes in Greek and English and is on the Board of Directors of 'Africa Peace University'.

Spiritual, inspirational, idealist, pacifist, Peace Ambassador, she believes that people and the environment will be healed only when Love and global peace prevails. Her poetry, political and visionary, deals with the themes of love, global peace, the environment, immediate ceasefire on all war fronts and education for all.

HOW THE CHILD GROWS HER LOVE FOR NATURE NATURALLY

As a child I grew up in an idyllic countryside environment surrounded by the sea, at a time when the word industrial pollution was unknown in the Greek islands. The island of Zakynthos where I grew up was pure and fresh at the time as it was 500 years before. The 100 year old houses in the historic village I grew up, almost as ancient as time, were built from pure materials; cement was totally unknown then. The walls of our home was at least 75 cm thick, to keep the house warm in winter and cool in the summer.

Porches had extra-large protective covered areas built in the right orientation, for morning and evening seating and family relaxation. Our home was our castle for our family and I was proud for its centurion origin. Home had its own garden where specific organic vegetables grew each season. I loved to plant them. Meat was a delicacy for special celebrations and seasons and was home produced. 10 minutes' walk on foot from home was the wine yard with its special varieties of seasonal vegetables and fruit trees. Along its long footpaths, wild scented roses and lavender shrubs, thyme and rosemary bushes were the delights of my childhood. I had my secret areas which I visited alone to find rare orchids and wild honeycombs to suckle, to dream and learn the perfect rhythms of nature. Delighted by the celebration of colors, fruits, vegetables and crops throughout the year, I also discovered the mystery of the sky, different and varied in castellation every night and experienced the awe of God by admiring the sky's blessed colors. Thus, I followed the traditions of my forefathers ceremoniously. The clarity and multi-blue brightness of the star lit sky is one of the most important experiences in my life. God was a daily experience, made more real with my grandmother's improvised stories of creation.

So it became natural to me to plant my own flower garden at home at the age of eight and found a way to care about it when I went on summer holidays. It was also natural for me to start a large school garden at the age of ten, my love for flowers and color combinations was what I now consider a divine gift, but did not realize it at the time. After I fully planted our school garden it never crossed my mind why other schoolgirls or boys of my age did not help me, despite my admonition to do so. This was a happy beginning of living in nature for nature and me, my love experience with the environment. Our school garden was damaged five times by floods and wild winds but I never gave up. In time I learnt that replanting life follows perhaps similar rules. One makes another brave optimistic fresh start. I now wonder where I found the courage and the new plants every time I started to plant from the beginning our new school garden. I wonder why I never was disappointed, defeated, lost faith or it never crossed my mind that a new garden could perhaps have the same possibilities to be lost under flooded water and mud. Optimism starts from the heart from lack of fear.

My next junior environmental project was to plant a pine trees wood in the barren area of the school yard. For this, I had volunteers who were my friends at school both boys and girls. It was at no time that hundred pine trees were planted with hope in celebration. It came naturally to me as I was looking after the pine trees, eager to see the growth of these future pine woods. I decided to water the pine trees rather than playing during the school breaks. This is how my long love for nature started and blossomed and it is more than a serious part of my life up to now.

As this teenager girl grew into a high school student and then a young woman, the environment acquired a stronger serious place in my life. I will now turn the "I" of my youth into the "she" of the mature woman who always worked hard to maintain, protect and teach the value of the environment to my son, students, and friends and widely to citizens of our planet.

SELECTIVE VOLUNTARY ENVIRONMENTAL CAMPAIGNS IN ENGLAND AND GREECE

- As high school student, she took the initiative to organize the planting of hundred eucalyptus trees, in a treeless area along the long road to hospital, in the town of Zakynthos, island of Zakynthos.
- In West Yorkshire, England, as environmental activist, she took the initiative and co-operated with the "Friends of the Earth" to investigate the dangers for a large rural coal mining community from considerable methane gas emissions caused by the rubbish it was deposited there for years in a long disused hollow area, 3 meters deep railway track. Finally, the tripping stopped due to the dangers diagnosed after investigation.
- Organised an environmental campaign in co-operation with the local Member of Parliament, an environmental film producer, local Councillors, environmental specialists. In the campaign the General secretary for the environment in West Yorkshire was very positively involved, as well as students, lecturers and long suffering local people to investigate the severe pollution caused by the largest public factory cleaning mined coal to smokeless coal in Barnsley, South Yorkshire. She preciously consulted and took the advice of local family Doctors for the statistics of respiratory diseases in the area, which were far above national average. As a result, a pollution measuring station was placed in the school grounds of the main village and the statistics about the air pollutants were made for the first time ever, available to the public in the central City Library.
- Additionally, she and her team together with the Secretary for the environment visited and inspected the large coke factory. After checking records, it was found that a much higher than permitted number of "coal ovens" to make it into smokeless coal were

treated during the night thus the air pollution was not seen during the night, neither the inhabitants of the area smelted the severe stench out of the huge factory chimneys. Luckily, it was found out that a European directive about air pollution was expected to be publicised and become into effect six months after their visit. The factory then was obliged by law to use special filters to reduce considerably the excessive air pollutants emitted from the factory chimneys during day, and night in particular.

- She subsequently contacted more family Doctors in the surrounding coalmining areas, which had much above average environmental pollution and gave them statistics about environmental pollutants and further respiratory diseases in those areas.

- Also she co-operates about key environmental issues in Greece, Kenya and Africa with a leading African environmentalist, who is a Lead Environmental Impact Assessment and Auditor Expert, Professor, Dr. Jared Akama Onyari, in Nairobi, Kenya, who is founder of " Kenya Environmental and Waste Management Association". Prof. Onyari is also affiliated with the United Nations Environmental Program (UNEP).

- She has contacted the leading Indian Professor Jaydeep Sharangi, who is leading the field "POETRY IN THE ENVIRONMENT" to look further into advancing Poetry readings and learning in the environment.

- In Athens, Greece her major environmental campaign for almost 7 years was about radiation caused from mobile phone aerials. She spotted a large mast of a mobile phone area in a low height building in the centre of a densely populated area in South Athens. She also discovered a specialist Professor in molecular biology at Athens University who started to measure the radiation 10 - 350 m away from the aerial, in the city square. A nursery school, a large primary school, the adjacent park, the senior citizens centre, multitude of shops and multi storey buildings, all were affected by the radiation. She also contacted the leading journalists in the Greece, who had international experience on mobile phone aerials radiation at a time when many dozens of people had died because they lived near Mobile phone aerials areas.

The professor's students, including his family, were out in the streets and visiting houses measuring daily the radiation. 99% of the local citizens ignored even the existence of the aerial. At least three people had developed serious types of cancer 30m away from the aerial, among which the daughter of a judge. We took the matter up to the council, collected considerable number of signatures but the council refused initially to discuss the matter publicly until we found that there were not legal permits issued for the installation of the aerials. We took the matter to the High court and won, including legal compensation. The compensation was never paid but we obliged through the council the telephone company to replace the old types of three mobile phone aerials with a modern one emitting less radiation. Our suspicions that the telephone company has given money under the table to the major and local councillors were beyond any doubts. The council did not reply to our letters and we came to a dead-end. Our gain was that the mayors of local nearby boroughs started similar campaigns and court cases, as well as in other far away municipalities of Attica, where 6 million people live. We are still waiting for the final court decision. We learnt though serious lessons, the judges are not adequately aware about the seriousness of damage to the body and number of deaths caused by radiation from high frequency mobile phone aerials. Corruption abounds. Doctors and teachers are not aware of the dangers. An amateur environmentalist has to do specialized international research to argue with public bodies, and it is time consuming. People ignore the obvious and sometimes they may never know that they may be victims too.

Poems by Roula Pollard

1. A TREE, ALWAYS IN MY MEMORY

I am in the memory, like the rings of a tree,
as you are in my memory.
I am not yours, you are not mine
only oneness in love. I have no possessions.

A tree I am.
This tree is not yours, nor mine
our life is a tree
valuable as our shared planet, valuable as oneness
in wholeness on this planet. Sea breezes
unite us, like a sea soul
even sadness is shared
in the body of our Universe.
Usually, I say " I gave up sadness"
turned it into an endless song
long as the days of my life
united by a delicate cotton thread with you
or by the strongest ropes, like those anchoring boats
on the pier, or long islands of the soul
visited in summertime.
United, yes, by a hyper-lexicon of love words
united by all trees to create life's oxygen
united by all hopes like a rising dawn
united by strong, powerful links
of world love and world peace.

2. HAS NATURE LOST ITS WAY?

When on long nights, I hear sudden cries perhaps coming
out
from white pillow feathers, do you exist in the same world
my friend, in which continent do you live?
Are the nights strange there too, blending with yellow
like swollen pieces of sky hanging from the ceiling
in the next room, or from your dreams?
Are the days confused like drunken birds in the sky?
There are some white days too
pure white without illusion
mixed with pollution.

Over - polluted environment
gives birth to white days
mixed with a sea of lies
in the United Lies corporation
with white and dark.
Where is the unlimited
truth hidden?

If you go to the beach today, my friend,
greet the sea, ask her for forgiveness too
for my silence and your ignorance,
you know the waves
are searching
for their peace.

Poems by Rashika Shaikh

Bio: Rashika Mohd Ismail Shaikh is a 20-year old English literature undergraduate from B. K. Birla College. She believes that poetry is a sublime form of self-expression.

1. The Woman

You are an eternal creation
A masterpiece of divine
Evolved from his rib
A diamond from coal mine.

Trust your competence
Face the crowd
Your story tell aloud
Make yourself proud.

Your beauty resembles rose
And strength its thorns
Outwardly though mimosa
Inwardly a mighty storm.

2. Worth yourself

Voice like a thunder
Stand beside him
Don't you surrender
Be composed within.

If water, food, oxygen
Keeps man alive
No denial to the fact
You give him life.

Neither a blotch
Nor the doom,
You are the sunshine
That makes flowers bloom.

Poems by Sangeeta Sharma

1. Niagara Falls:

They stole my heart away
Breath-taking, bewitching
Majestic and mesmerizing!
Flowing with the racy waters
Miles together
I rose and ebbed
I sighed and swayed
Moaned and heaved
Cascading down from the heights
Hitting below the boulders
Sprung up high as the spray
Sprinkled across the bay
Ensconced again in the depths
Again rollicking to the roar
Gyrating with the waves
Waltzing on the rainbow
What oomph!
Wowed and crazed
Gave my heart away!!!

2. Halcyon:

A voluptuous lake rests

Under the wooden bridge
Wide expanse of aquamarine
Till the reach of the eye
You gaze at it and gaze
Ceaseless, spellbound
Sipping droughts not of water
But of the enrapturing sight

Senses loosen,
Unwind
You feel healed and unbound
By the panoramic view
For more and more you crave
Under the open azure sky

Blue expanse ahead
And
Blue expanse above
Velvety sappherine clots
Making a slow movement
In the sky
The super beatific sight!

Looking aloft and below
Is healing, inspiring
Heavenly
An epiphany:
Nature is Truth
And Truth, Nature

Nothing beyond
And Nothing beside!

3. Peacock

Not just one
It was a pair:
A peacock, a peahen
Walking and pecking in the grass
Of a plush neighbourhood.

It was sheer delight
To gawk at
The most beautiful bird
Colourful with oodles of grace

From such close quarters
With her shimmering blue and green plumage

The peahen takes a flight and
Settles on a branch
Of a *jamun* tree
Adorning the iridescent head crown
 Epitome of grace, pride, and beauty

But lo!
Suddenly drops from the tree
And instantly attacked by a dog below
The other develops tremors
And its neck twists.

In adherence to biosecurity measures:
Insecticides and herbicides,
Encroachment, poaching
And scarcity of water-
the main causes
Of the plummeting numbers
Calls for conservation measures.

Editor's Bio

Dr. Sangeeta Sharma

Dr. Sangeeta Sharma is a widely published critic, poet and writer.

In 2012, she authored a book on Arthur Miller, an anthology on poetry and another collection of 76 poems in 2017. She has jointly edited five anthologies on poetry, fiction and criticism. A freelance journalist, she currently heads the department of English, B. K. Birla College of Arts, Science and Commerce (Autonomous), Kalyan, Mumbai Metropolitan Region.

She is recognized as a PhD Guide in English Literature by the University of Mumbai.

Under Faculty Exchange Programme, she twice visited the University Department of English, Clayton State University, Georgia, USA, in March-April 2012 and 2014.

In 2014, she presented a research paper on Arthur Miller in the 38th Comparative Drama Conference, Baltimore, M.D., U.S.A.

In 2016, she led a delegation of college-students to Tianjin University of Technology, Tianjin,
China.

In May 2019, she participated as a poet and organizing secretary of 'Setu' international Bilingual literary fest held in Toronto, Canada.

Email ID: drsharma.sangeeta@gmail.com
Phone: 9769996948
Address: 502, 'A' Type, 'A' Wing, Umapati Building, Madhav-Srishti Complex, Godrej Hill Road, Khadakpada, Kalyan-West, Mumbai.

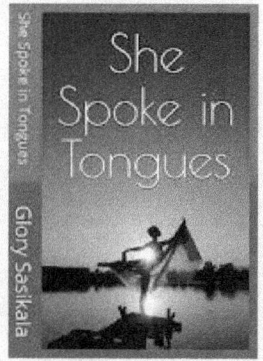

She Spoke in Tongues :: Glory
Sasikala

Paco's Atlas And Other Poems
By John Thieme

Ps-Fs :: Sunil Sharma

छोटी सी बात (लघुकथा संग्रह)
अनुराग शर्मा

India as an IT Superpower
Anurag Sharma

अनुरागी मन कथा संग्रह :: लेखक: अनुराग शर्मा

आग से अंतरिक्ष तक :: अज़ीज़ राय

Basic Hindi 2 Workbook :: Sonia Taneja

Setu Publications, Pittsburgh (USA)

Contact: setuedit@gmail.com